Liao Hor
Fragments of a Life

From Changting to Norwich

⋈

Innes Herdan

Larks Press

Published by the Larks Press
Ordnance Farmhouse, Guist Bottom, Dereham NR20 5PF
01328 829207

in association with
Innes Herdan
81A, Gloucester Avenue, London NW1 8LB

and
Derek Bryan
6, Southgate Lane, Bracondale, Norwich NR1 2DB

This book may be obtained from any of the three addresses above.

Printed by the Lanceni Press, Fakenham.

British Library Cataloguing-in-Publication Data
A catalogue record for this book is available in the British Library.

ISBN 0 948400 45 5

CONTENTS

ILLUSTRATIONS

Preface

Liao Hongying is my close friend of College days - that time of extraordinary openness, when we explored our ideas and emotions with a great deal of freedom and few inhibitions. A never-to-be-repeated time. Our lives continued together for a short while in China; a mere six months. Her later years had to be recovered from intermittent meetings, sometimes at long intervals; her childhood from her own memories. And we all know how these remain in our consciousness in a rather unbalanced mix.

What prompted me to put all this together was my awareness that here was a quite remarkable human being, and one who exemplified in her thinking the flow of events in a particularly intense period of development in the Far East. From these two points of view it seemed to me that her life merited record.

Hongying's antecedents were by no means exceptional. She was born in a small town in Southern China, of a family poor in worldly goods but where book-learning was idolized, as it tended to be in the old Chinese culture. The men of her household were scholars, in the Confucian sense; the women did women's work - cooking, sewing and embroidery, washing and cleaning. Only Hongying didn't fit into this pattern.

Her mother had wanted a boy. As if in answer to this wish, Hongying developed some of the attributes of a traditional male, uncommon in a Chinese girl of that time (the early twentieth century): determination, strong will, intellectual curiosity. And she escaped the household chores as a little girl and heartily disliked them to the end of her days. Her father, who died when she was barely fourteen, tried to develop in her a love of the classical texts which were his bread of life. He also introduced her to ancient poetry. This she wasn't able to respond to, but subconsciously it seems to have opened up a parallel love of music, particularly Western symphonic music, much later when she came to England. "It makes life so different", she wrote to me, "sweeter, and more enduring and richer altogether."

But her life was not destined to develop in a calm environment. The missionary schools which she attended brought her into contact with advanced ideas, Western ideas, and history supplied the catalyst. With her hot enthusiasm she threw herself into the revolutionary struggle so vehemently that her life was eventually in danger and she was advised to escape to England. This sealed her destiny, ensuring that she would spend her life between China and England, never quite coming to rest. She lived, in fact, in two worlds and didn't entirely fit into either. This is evident in the way she uses language. Though she has spent rather more of her long life in England, Chinese remains the language of deep familiarity for her. Yet with her English husband, who speaks Chinese with ease, she converses sometimes in one, sometimes the other, sometimes uses both in the same sentence. This must indicate something about the way she thinks and feels. And this is the story I have tried to tell in these next pages.

I have called it 'Fragments of a Life'. Liao Hongying has lived so long that many of her contemporaries cannot tell their tales any more - they have gone to join the Yellow Emperor. And she herself only remembers certain parts in any detail. As I write this, she is almost 90. Her letters to me, vivid and thoughtful, revived memories; the contents of her notebooks added pungent details. I spoke or corresponded with a number of her friends - those who are still living. But all this only left me with 'fragments' of a long life.

Born at the end of the Chinese Empire, she has lived through the Republic of Sun Yatsen, the warlords and Chiang Kaishek, the Civil War and the founding of the People's Republic - a big chunk of history. She has seen her country emerge from foreign domination into an independent modern power with a hopeful future. So hers is, on the whole, a happy story, though like every human life, it has had to take the blows of fate.

I couldn't have written this without the help of her husband, Derek Bryan. He filled in many details, kept me on the right track and checked the whole typescript while remaining unobtrusively in the background.

Of Hongying's friends, I should like to thank particularly Kate Allan, Ranjana and William Ash, Beth Bailey, Joan Browne, Margaret Griffith, Enid Huws Jones, Peter Lisowski and Gladys Yang for their recollections. I am also grateful to John Lloyd for so admirably setting out the political background of the British organisations concerned with China with which Hongying was chiefly involved for almost 40 years.

The illustrations reproduced here are from a variety of sources, many of them no longer traceable. To those of the photographers who are still living, I should like to offer my thanks

London
December 1994.

iii

Family group in the old home, taken 31 July 1975, on the occasion of Hongying's first return to Changting with her husband.
Her eldest brother is seated between them, with his wife on far left and her third brother's widow on far right.

Part 1. Childhood

Hongying was born on 24 December 1905, into the family of a poor but highly-respected Confucian scholar. The two characters of her name meant 'great hero' (heroine); her father avoided the soft feminine names usually reserved for girls and expressed his wish for a daughter with the bold fighting spirit she in fact exemplified all her life. These were the last years of the Empire, the end of the already enfeebled Qing dynasty.

1905 was also the year of Japan's victory over Russia (the Russo-Japanese war), the first defeat of a Western power by an Eastern one, and of the attempted Russian Revolution, which was to work like leaven among the dissatisfied youth of China. So Hongying was born at a turning point in Chinese history. Her birthplace, Changting, a small town in the interior of Fujian province, at the foot of the great Wuyi mountain range, was little touched by what was going on in the wider world: the women were engrossed in family affairs; the men in securing a living. Hongying's ancestors had lived and been buried there for many generations. This province was one of the poorest in China and her home was in one of the poorest and most educationally backward parts. Hongying's mother used to say that just as a table had four legs, a woman should have four sons. In old China, girls were not considered important, but the more boys, the more meritorious. Only boys could carry on the ancestor worship and pray for their parents when they died.

Hongying's parents had had five sons, but one died in infancy and another as a young child. When her sister was born next, that was bad enough, but when Hongying appeared - another girl - so great was her mother's disappointment that she refused to feed her at the breast. But her father was a tender-hearted person. He took a little spoon and fed her on rice water, saying that even if he had ten daughters, he would keep them all alive. In poor families - and hers was poor - it was not uncommon then to drown baby girls at birth or sell them. Girls needed husbands and that meant dowries. After a while and grudgingly, her mother began to suckle her. Hongying went on sucking, even when there was no more milk, for a very long time, so long that she made a hole in her mother's dress. They told her that when she was tiny, she had slept with her face pressed against her mother's breast, and this was the source of her flat nose!

A baby's horoscope was an important matter in China and Hongying's was not good. The time, day and month of her birth were submitted to an astrologer but he gave a gloomy report: she wouldn't have a younger brother - there would be no more boys - she would cause harm to her parents and to her husband, and her destiny was inauspicious. In fact, she had not been born under a good star, but since she was the baby of the family, they all (except the mother) loved her dearly and she was very much spoilt. She was the *manzi* of the family - the last and most loved. Her brothers used to tease her, saying that she wasn't her mother's child but had been bought and came in a little basket, slung from a shoulder-pole. "But all my children came in baskets!" said her mother. There was a lot of good-humoured teasing. They all loved her so much and when she was young, they made a very happy family (before the arrival of daughters-in-law, that is).

When Hongying was about three years old and had learnt to talk, her father took her on his lap and tried to teach her to recite some simple Tang dynasty poems. It was quite easy for her to learn by heart but she naturally had no idea of the meaning. After a while, her second brother (Er-Ge), who specially loved her, noticed that although she seemed intellectually gifted, she showed no enthusiasm for this parrot-like recitation. He asked his father to let him take charge of Hongying's education. Their father was quite happy with this arrangement which left him free to concentrate on teaching classical Chinese to the dozen or so young men who came individually to his home for their lessons.

At this time, when she was still quite young, she had to practise writing, using tracing paper over printed Chinese characters. When she grew older, she had to write these elaborate characters freely, with brush and ink, every morning till her wrist ached. Written Chinese plays such an important part in the culture, - much more than with the alphabetic languages. Each character represents an object or concept, each with its own associations, so that to look at a page of characters rouses many thoughts and stimulates the imagination. China's written language, far more than any alphabetic script can be, is a key to an understanding of its country's culture and history.

Hongying's father taught her and her sister together at first. The sister, who was four years older, used to sit on a stool at his feet. Though she tried hard, she never managed to progress, so she was handed over to her mother to be instructed in sewing, embroidery and cooking, all the preparations for marriage when she would be old enough. In fact, she was married at 15 or 16.

Their father was indeed a broad-minded person, for in those days girls were not generally considered worth educating at all. In the whole county, only one other girl besides Hongying succeeded in acquiring enough book knowledge to go to high school, something not easy for us to

3

imagine. Hongying was steadily learning the Classics by heart, for instance the *Hundred Surnames* and the *Three Character Classic* (*San Zi Jing*), a Primer of three-character sentences. This was the regular Confucian style education of the time.

Grandmother's care

Since her early childhood, her paternal grandmother had played an important role in Hongying's life. As a tiny child, she used to sleep with her parents, father at one end of the bed and mother at the other, but when she grew bigger, she slept with her grandmother.

The grandmother's and grandfather's bed was a very poor one, made of bamboo with a base of boards and a straw mattress, but her parents had a big four-poster - the bed for the marriage of the eldest son, and then the second son when he got a wife; in fact the marriage bed.

When sleeping with her grandmother, Hongying slept so soundly that Er-Ge had to come and shake her; sometimes the only way to make her stir was to put a cold wet facecloth over her face. Till her twenties, she always slept like this - so deeply she could hardly be woken - they thought she must have the sleeping sickness. After Er-Ge had roused her, he washed her face and brushed her hair. She had rather short, brownish hair (not the glossy black which most Chinese have). This was when she was a little girl, but even when she was older, he used to comb and plait it for her every morning. He loved this little sister so much and did everything he could for her, and she adored him.

Hongying was terrified of ghosts! In her very young days, so she told me, her grandmother used to sit on her parents' bed when she was going to sleep and tell her ghost stories (from the *Liao Zhai*, translated by Giles as *Strange Stories from a Chinese Studio*). The fox fairies and the bad spirits! She was so frightened! It never occurred to her that they were literary inventions. She used to pull the covers over her head so as not to see a ghost. The ancestral portraits that hung in the downstairs hall, looking so solemn to a child, their faces so severe - scared her too. She was afraid of seeing them peering out at her in the darkness. Of course the whole house was full of shadows. Their only light was from a pewter oil lamp with a rush in it. They would only burn two rushes at a time; if they took three rushes, their mother complained that it used too much oil.

Er-Ge who cared for her so much, must have realised her terror. "There are no such things as ghosts (*gui*)" he said. "Come upstairs and sleep in my room". Hongying loved being there with him - there was no more need to cover her head and she felt completely at ease. Many years later, when she was at boarding school, and one of the girls died of diphtheria - which was a deadly disease then, especially in a backward country like China - her old fears reawakened. She was afraid of seeing the ghost of the dead girl! She often had a feeling that this ghost was standing behind her.

Family home

A board, hung in the place of honour in their home, in the County Town of Changting (the Prefecture of Tingzhou) read: '*Liao Wen De Tang*' - The cultured and virtuous Liao family hall. Because Hongying's father was the only Liao scholar of his generation, the clan had chosen him to live in this large family building and care for it. The traditional

Chinese style house was mostly of one storey, built round a courtyard, with small trees or plants to make it green and shady; the whole family would spend a lot of their time there in the heat of the summer. When the family expanded, another section and another courtyard were added on for the newly-weds. The original Liao home had been almost completely burnt down when Hongying was a baby. The present house was in three sections with two courtyards and a small central hall which had an upper storey; this was where Er-Ge slept and studied. On the West side of the house were the children's and the mother's room; on the East side, the kitchen and Granny's room. There were two halls, one of which had a wall covered with a map of the First World War; Er-Ge had pinned little flags on it to show the position of the armies. On the opposite wall were the orange-red slips of paper announcing her brothers' successes in the government examinations. There were very few books in the house apart from the Classics, in old bindings - no modern novels or modern books of any kind. The value of education and learning in the old China simply took precedence over every other activity, and this evaluation stayed with Hongying all her life. In writing to a friend a few years ago she says: "Have I got it right, that you have four children? It is amazing that you managed to give them all good education, and the same to the grandchildren. What an achievement! In China your house would be [regarded as] a large household with the title of Honoured Family bestowed as it, written on red paper, pasted on the lintel of your door, and scrolls on either side forming a couplet with auspicious meaning".

There was a yard outside which must have seemed huge to young children. Hongying remembers its three peach trees, the mass of pink flowers in Spring, so lovely against the general greyness. Behind the house was a playground with mulberry trees - also huge; the children used to play there under the trees. The main street ran along the front of the house, sloping from South to North, a long straight cobbled road. On each side were ditches which filled with spring water when the rains came; little lively fish swam in it. The children liked to catch them and tip them into the big urn in the front garden where their father kept goldfish - the kind with protruding eyes and white tails; Hongying used to pick special leaves to feed them but, when their father died the children no longer cared for them. The road changed its character in later years: after the Revolution, it was all cemented over to make it easier to clean - the ditches have gone, the cobbles have gone, it has all been tidied up. Of course it is more healthy, but something has been lost as well.

At the North end of this road was a temple, dedicated to Guan Di, whose grounds Hongying also loved to explore as a child. It was overgrown with all kinds of weeds and wild plants and had a pond where water chestnuts floated; there were fish in it too. To Hongying the whole place seemed so calm and beautiful.

But the temple itself was a different matter. The Guan Di who presided over it was variously worshipped as the God of War, protector of the Empire, and patron of merchants and scholars. He was based on a real person named Guan Yu, a loyal and heroic soldier who had fought in the wars of the Three Kingdoms in the third century A.D. He was given the title of 'Di' (Supreme Being) at the end of the 16th century and became a popular god, worshipped throughout China. His portrait was pasted up here at the main gateway; to Hongying he was a fierce, even ferocious figure. Below him was the picture of the first level of the Buddhist Hell. They were burning people in oil! She couldn't bear to look at them! Inside the temple, she remembered, there were two effigies from Buddhist legend, a tall one (Gao Ye) and a short (Ai Ye). Once a year they were paraded through the streets: wherever they were to pass, each household put out tables with incense, candles and one or three dishes of food. It was a lively event, all the children rushing out of their homes and running behind in crowds.

Across the street from the Liaos' was a gateway behind which many families lived, in a long, low building; they were very interesting to Hongying and she loved going there to the gateway to watch them. One of the neighbour's wives had bars across her bedroom window and it was rumoured that she entertained men friends. This was wonderfully mysterious and wicked to Hongying! These families were mostly peasants or artisans or people in trade, and Confucius had looked down on manual labour and despised working for money. She was not allowed to play with any of their children; they were all illiterate and lacked the culture which her father was intent on teaching her. Theirs was a family of scholars with a reputation to keep up; he didn't want her to learn anything bad from them. In fact, she and her brothers and sisters felt rather isolated. They never heard the clink of mahjong tiles, for instance, as in so many of the houses round about. Mahjong, so popular and widespread in the old China, was a gambling game and her father had told his sons, "No drinking, no smoking (of cigarettes, much less opium), no gambling, no concubines", so they did not come into contact with any of these things in their daily lives.

One very beautiful young woman from one of the houses opposite used to carry Hongying about. She loved her more than her own sister - adored her in fact. One day

8

they saw her being carried away in a sedan-chair. There was a trade in pretty girls and young women between Fujian, where Hongying's hometown was, and Guangdong province to the South; a man engaged in this trade must have carried her off to be a concubine, or simply a prostitute. Hongying cried and cried but they never heard of her again.

Further along the street to the South was the big house of Ma the merchant and his family. This was where the opium-smoking and gossip went on; of course Hongying was not allowed to go there either - not to be in contact with their bad habits. But she watched the women standing outside their gates and chattering after their husbands had gone off to work. Then came the houses where the small tradespeople lived, illiterate but somehow managing to earn enough for their food.

The older generation

Her family's isolation was only broken by occasional visits from relatives living in other parts of the country. Father's elder sister, for instance, had been married as a baby into a peasant family - that is, she had been betrothed 70 *li* away (3 *li* are approximately 1 mile). Once a year, at the Lunar New Year, she and her son used to visit the Liaos, bringing sweet potatoes and vegetables from their land. Hongying specially loved the sweet potatoes - thought them wonderful! This cousin used to take a puppet-show all round the neighbouring villages as part of the New Year festivities. Hongying's mother always produced two pairs of shoes for them, one for her sister-in-law and one for the son, made by her own daughters-in-law. Hongying always remembered the drawers at home, stuffed with bits of cotton material, saved by her mother for making the shoe soles. These were real rags - old clothes torn up or bits left from her third brother's tailoring trade. The pieces were always in a jumble and it was one of Hongying's particular pleasures to sort and tidy them. She always had a strong sense of order; for many years she collected interesting pebbles, arranging them according to size, colour, type. Even in later years, she goes on looking for such stones in the gravel outside her front door in Norwich, where she and her husband came to spend their old age.

Her father's younger sister was said to have been a great beauty, though Hongying was too young to remember her when they lived in Changting. She was married to a Manchu, a high military official, who lived in the garrison headquarters, a few minutes walk south of the Liao household. To marry this lovely woman must have cost the husband's family a great deal. But the Liao family was criticised during the 1911 Revolution for having married a daughter to a Manchu. Perhaps because the marriage was frowned on, the couple left Changting and went back to live at his home in Fuzhou; after her husband died, only Hongying's eldest brother remembered anything about this aunt. When Hongying was in Fuzhou some years ago, she had no means of tracing her.

As for Hongying's paternal grandparents, her grand-father was illiterate, which left Grandma free of the social conventions such as her mother had to follow (as the wife of a scholar). Grandpa had joined the Taiping Rebellion (1850-1865) when he was about 16 or 17; when the rebellion ended he got a job looking after a rich man's orchard. But even this was too much for him; he gave it up and bought four goats, and was content just to herd them. He was not a very forceful personality or particularly able, and in fact Grandma,

10

who was an extremely independent woman, was known to despise him. She fell in love with a Liao cousin, a scholar, and this was how they came to have such an intelligent father. Long after, her eldest brother told Hongying the story.

Grandma was already in her 60s when Hongying was born, so in the years when Hongying remembers her, she didn't have to do any of the cooking or housework; she was perfectly free and went about wherever she liked. She used to go by herself to the nearest shopping centre, and because she was very sociable, she would chat with all the other women there, and the young male shop assistants. When Hongying was really little, Grandma used to carry her on her back; later she trotted along behind her wherever she went. She still remembers those shops, she says - the rice, the soya sauce, the vinegar and oil, the special smell of the spices.

Hongying's parents

Hongying's father, Liao Xiuyan, was a true scholar. Vaguely she remembers, when a very small child, that once a year, on Confucius' birthday, he put on his gorgeous long robes, embroidered with dragon and phoenix, and went to the Confucian temple at midnight. A solemn ceremony took place there before dawn, with an ox and goats being sacrificed (pork wasn't good enough for the gods of heaven and earth, and mutton was thought to have a rank smell). The scholars returned in the early morning, bringing a large piece of beef. (Some people thought beef was too tough, but in her family, meat was rare and they didn't mind!) In years long after, when writing to a sister-in-law who had sent her a ginger cake, Hongying explained that "I am used to 'ginger food' [as] Confucius never had a meal without ginger. My father was 110% follower of this most divine philosopher-teacher, so we were brought up on 'ginger food', though we were so poor that we nearly always felt hungry".

The embroidery design on the robes varied according to the wearer's degree in the Imperial Examination system. Hongying's father, although a good scholar, had always refused to become an official, saying it was 'dirty'. But she remembers his going to the provincial capital, Fuzhou, to take the Imperial Examination for *juren* (the second degree, higher then *xiucai*). He was taken ill on the journey but a message was passed back to him: ('Your name is already known to the Imperial Court's Literary Department') and he was given an equivalent award.

About these robes, Hongying explained how the buckles were worn at the centre-front, the two ends coupled together like a snake's-head belt The central government had departments for making robes, buckles, and all the other finery; they could not be bought anywhere else. It was not only the men who wore these splendid robes; their wives did as well, and when they died, they wore them in the coffin. Hongying's parents died in their fifties, within a year of each other, when she was about 14.

The children never knew what their parents died of because they could not afford to have one of the two local doctors (trained in the London Missionary Society's* Hospital) till it was too late. The local herbalist prescribed strychnine for the father when he was dying. The whole family took turns to watch over him; all were horrified for he died a very painful death.

*When she later came to England and saw LMS (London Midland and Scottish, the old regional railway company) written on the hoardings, she mistook it for 'London Missionary Society', and thought what an important institution that must be!

In old China, the coffin had to be kept in the house for seven times seven days before the funeral (though some were kept much longer because the relations were too poor to afford the funeral rites). All this time, the relations and local people of good social position came to pay their tribute to the deceased. The women had to cry loudly every night (ritual wailing); the men just bowed. When the women wailed for her father, Hongying did too, but hers were real tears - her father had meant so much to her. This was one of the great and lasting griefs of her life.

Although the Manchu dynasty in its later years had abolished the old system of appointing officials through Imperial Examination in the Chinese classics, and was supposed to have set up schools on the Western pattern, there were so few in the whole County, they could only cater for a few children: boys of better-off families or who were exceptionally bright. Some fathers still sent their sons to be taught Classical Chinese by private tutors. So before the Liao boys were old enough to earn, their father taught young men the *Four Books* and some of the *Five Classics**. He would teach them individually, then they would recite in unison, seated side by side on benches. On Feast Days, they brought presents of meat. Also in the days of the Empire, scholars with good handwriting would be asked to write large characters on scrolls, to hang in temples or the walls of private houses. They received 'presents' for this in the form

*The classical canon which formed the basis of instruction in old China consisted of the Four Books (*Si Shu*): the *Great Learning*, the *Doctrine of the Mean*, the *Analects of Confucius* (a record of his sayings) and the *Sayings of Mencius* (Confucius' disciple), and the *Five Classics* (*Wu Jing*): *Book of Songs*, *Book of History*, *Book of Changes*, *Book of Rites* and the *Spring and Autumn Annals*.

of money. So their father's writing and teaching were what the whole family lived by, somewhat precariously, till the sons were old enough to earn. (When Hongying returned to Changting in 1959, she saw some of her father's writing in the family's clan temple.)

Everybody in the town knew the head of the Liao family. Whenever he was coming home, as soon as he reached the temple at the north end of the road, the children in the whole neighbourhood would rush to surround him. When she heard this commotion, she always knew he was coming and would rush to meet him. He loved all these children and treated them all, dirty and snotty-nosed as they might be, as if they were his own. He was so much respected that if anyone had a dispute with a neighbour, he or she would bring it to him to settle. For this reason he was often late in getting back.

In 1959, on her first return to the family home for over 30 years, Hongying stopped somewhere on the way to Changting for lunch. A young woman remarked to her that she 'looked different' and asked who she was. Hongying told her briefly where she had come from and asked whether this woman had ever heard of her father. She replied with enthusiasm "of course we all know his name!" The ordinary people knew him so well - and also his eldest son.

Her father had no sense of money - how to plan or save or manage a household. He was a real absent-minded scholar. Often he would take a lantern in the evening and go to the Poetry Club, where a few scholars would meet together to compose poems or cap verses. Sometimes they would recite poems of the Tang - the great age of Chinese poetry. This was his deepest interest and he wanted to share it with his little daughter, but it was of no use - the only time Hongying went with him to his group, she fell asleep. In

14

later years, she could see him in her mind's eye - crossing a bridge over the river and carrying a glass lantern lit by a candle.

As a scholar's wife, Hongying's mother never went out of doors to mix with other people except when relatives or friends were getting married. Then, in grand official robes, she would be invited to be matron-of-honour*. This was because she had sons and because her horoscope had showed that she was someone with an auspicious destiny and so would bring luck to the bride. She was carried to the wedding feast in a sedan chair with curtains round it, and sometimes she took Hongying with her as a small child. Hongying didn't particularly enjoy these outings. One of her clearest memories, and a rather unpleasant one, was of eating fish at the banquet and disliking it because of the bones! To this day, she is wary of eating fish!

The only other occasion that Hongying can remember when her mother ventured into the street was when her eldest brother fell ill (the eldest son was regarded as of special importance for carrying on the family) and her mother visited a Buddhist temple to pray for his recovery. Since her father disapproved of Buddhism, he didn't allow his wife to visit temples in the ordinary way, but this was an exception. Of

* In his autobiographical story, *Beneath the Red Banner* (Eng. trans. Don J. Cohn, Panda Books, Beijing), the writer Lao She also describes his mother's attending weddings and funerals as a 'matron-of-honour'. "A widow, a woman born in a Tiger Year, or a woman whose behaviour was not exemplary did not qualify...Only respectable matrons could undertake this responsibility...Clothing and jewellery, needless to say, had to be more splendid than those of the other guests. My mother detested borrowing things, but she couldn't afford to buy a satin gown costing 20 or 30 ounces of silver, an overcoat with an embroidered border, pure gold brooches, earrings or hairpins. Having no alternative, she had to turn to my aunt for help."

course she didn't know how to go and Hongying had to act as guide. She offered incense, candles, firecrackers, little bowls of rice, chicken and wine, and prayed for her son's recovery. He did in fact recover. This was the only time that Hongying can remember when her mother went out of the house on foot apart from a short journey down the road to her school when she was ill with dysentery.

Hongying and her mother were never very close. Apart from that rejection at birth, which must have left a subconscious wound, Hongying simply found her dull. She had nothing interesting to talk about and did nothing particularly well. Before there were daughters-in-law, her only household work was a little cooking; she also washed clothes every day. In Hongying's familiar picture of her, she is bending over the washtub, rubbing and scrubbing. She used to starch some of their things - Hongying can still remember how stiff and uncomfortable they felt and how the collars tickled her neck. Still farther back, when she was even smaller, her mother used to carry in a wooden tub full of hot water every evening to bath her - or rather to wash her feet and bottom. Among the bride-gifts which Hongying remembers being brought to the bride's future home, with music and jubilation, the silks, bedspreads, quilts and so on, was this wooden tub. But her lasting recollection was of her mother's lack of understanding towards her daughters-in-law when they came into the family. She was always grumbling about them, and they in turn grumbled about her, and her sister grumbled about them all, so that there was very little harmony among the womenfolk as Hongying was growing up. Looking back, Hongying realises that the source of all her mother's complaints was the fact that she never had enough money. Many an evening her mother would ask Hongying what she would do when she was older. "Teach and earn money" was the reply. "What will you do with the money?" her mother would press her. "Give it to you!"

Brothers and Sister

Hongying's eldest brother (Da-Ge) was absolutely not interested in money either, he had no business sense. When his mother sent him shopping, he would come back with the wrong food, or only enough for one meal. Because of his learning and good character, he had been invited to occupy part of a Confucian temple; he had his study there and his school. Students came to him for private coaching, as they had done to his father, and those who came from a distance would stay for the night. Hongying loved staying there too - the air of the temple courtyard was so calm, quiet, orderly and beautiful. The small central hall and the siderooms became a sort of self-contained flat. No one collected the rent.

This brother was so much older than Hongying - 19 years, almost a generation - that they hardly had anything in common. It was not till much later that she came to appreciate his noble character, when he was an old man of over 80. In later life, she heard tales of his great spirit - how he had been persecuted in his old age, during the Cultural Revolution, how he had spoken up for those who were wrongly accused and secured their release: he had remained staunch, carrying on the spirit of his father. During the eighties she heard him praised all over the County town of Changting; when she read about him in the newly compiled local history, it was like reading about someone quite strange to her. He died in 1976, and the County authorities organised a big funeral to do him honour. In London, where she then was, Hongying composed an epitaph and cabled it to China. Despite this, she found, when she visited the tomb in 1979, that the gravestone bore only her nephews' names. Women were still considered unfit to take part in these solemn matters in the backward interior of the country. Hongying complained that it was 'feudal'.

Her second brother held a special place in her heart. Sixteen years older than her and already teaching in a Primary School, he was the one she profoundly admired and tried to model herself on. He really brought her up in the sense of learning and self-discipline. He taught her always to think honestly and never pretend. To this day, she still attributes much of her firmness and other qualities to his teaching and example. He had remarkably progressive ideas on education, more in line with the scientific spirit gradually creeping in from the West to even such a sheltered tradition-bound town as Changting. Noticing how receptive she was he soon began to teach her, not only the Classics, but general scientific knowledge, explaining in his own words and drawing diagrams. She remembers how he explained the solar system to her with candles. All her interest in intellectual matters came from him - a debt she feels she could never repay.

He had plenty of practical sense too. As soon as he began to earn, he took over the management of the household. He planned the expenditure: so much for rice, so much for vegetables and other essentials. He bought fuel, salt and grain in bulk - a whole sack of rice at a time, so there was no more misery at night with their mother shedding tears over the empty rice crock because there wasn't even enough to make a thin gruel for breakfast the next morning. The whole family ate regularly and better and more economically as well. It still grieves Hongying that his married life should

18

have turned out so unhappily. But this was later.

With her third brother (San-Ge) she had tremendous sympathy but somehow the two never became close. At some point in his schooling, he decided he didn't want to learn any more; he wanted to be a soldier, especially in the cavalry since he loved horses. Down the street, not far from their house, was the headquarters of a Manchu military commander; on either side of the entrance, two guards were stationed on horseback. San-Ge used to take Hongying there to look at the horses. He longed to enlist but his father absolutely forbade him. He really had a hard time; his father had no sympathy for someone who wasn't a scholar. In old China, scholars ranked highest in society - never mind whether they made money or not. After them came the farmers, the artisans and last the merchants (business people). The military were nowhere: 'good iron isn't used for nails; good sons don't become soldiers' is a well-known saying.

Hongying felt sure this brother would make a fine cavalry man. Whenever there was a local fair, he would hire a horse and let her ride in front of him. But although she enjoyed this and trusted him completely, she didn't really care about riding. She admits to having always been rather timid - even cowardly, in physical things; she was afraid of the sea, for instance, and never learnt to swim.

This brother was rather different from the other boys; because he was not devoted to book-learning, he developed in other ways. She remembers how he had a pigeon-cote and used to tie whistles under the pigeons' wings. He would take them up to the top of the hill and let them fly back, the sound of their whistles echoing round the sky. She always thought her father treated him unfairly because he had given up studying, but though he rebelled against conventional schooling, he had different gifts from his brothers, beautiful

19

handwriting, for instance.

The two elder boys succeeded really well in their comparatively modern studies. They both came first in their exams, one after the other, at the Teachers' Training College. The results were brought into the town with a band and drums and plenty of commotion. They must have considered this a mixed blessing however, as handsome tips were necessary for the 'musicians'!

They also passed well enough to be accepted for University, but they couldn't take up their places because the rest of the family had to be fed. Some other parents offered to pay all expenses for her second brother if he would attend University with their son and coach him. But it was no use: this boy was not quite at the right stage and Er-Ge had to begin earning and help to support the rest of them.

Marriages

It was not uncommon for a family to buy a baby girl, or a young girl, as the future wife for a son who was not yet born. The child had to leave her own home and was brought to live with her future husband's family, to whom, it was hoped, she would bring good luck, i.e. the wife would give birth to a son. As soon as she was old enough, she did all the housework, rather than the daughters and was really no more than a servant. The family saved a lot of money and gained cheap labour. If the mother-in-law was unsympathetic, the girl's life could be terribly hard. Suicides were not uncommon. In her family, Hongying always supported her sisters-in-law against the criticisms of her mother and sisters, and this led to quarrels.

Er-Ge's future wife was brought into the Liao house-

20

hold soon after she was born. Her father was an official named Guo, a scholar and a good friend of Hongying's father. This Guo had noticed her second brother when he was a little boy of three or four - that he seemed very bright. Guo's wife was pregnant at the time, so it was arranged that if the new baby turned out to be a girl, she should come to the Liao home to be Er-Ge's future wife. And so it happened. The baby girl was brought over when she was only about five days old.

The first wedding Hongying can remember was her eldest brother's. When a girl was about 15, the formal marriage usually took place. Da-Ge's bride was brought to the Liao household, carried in a sedan chair with red curtains (red being the colour of happiness). Hongying has no recollection of the wedding ceremony, only of the feast that followed - the tables in the hall loaded with food. She remembers the bridal chamber furniture and the nice smell of the newly-painted room. Her parent's bedroom was the only one with a wooden floor; the others were just beaten earth. They gave up this bedroom to the newly-weds and also the bridal bed which would be handed down through the generations.

So Da-Sao (eldest sister-in-law) came into the family. She was quite uneducated and Hongying began gradually to teach her, spending a lot of time with her. In China then, it wasn't considered proper for the new husband and wife to be too much together at first. In fact, there was no privacy in a Chinese household. In the beginning, Hongying spent most evenings teaching Da-Sao to read, then her husband took it on. He sent her to school and in time she herself became a Primary School teacher. She turned out to be quite clever, but she was a harsh person with no natural kindness. Her family was quite poor; her mother used to come and see her rather too often. Hongying's mother disagreed with this; she accused her daughter-in-law of giving away food and said that it wasn't right for her mother to make such frequent visits.

This Da-Sao was still alive when Hongying and her English husband came back to China for a visit in 1986. She was then 88 years old, the last living member of Hongying's generation, and no longer recognised anybody. As long as Da-Sao's husband lived, there had been harmony in the family, but after he died and she took over as family head, there was nothing but squabbling - as so often happens.

As for the wife of Hongying's second brother, when she grew up, the family ignored her and her husband could not bear her. She was crushed all her life, with no chance to develop. The family seldom had enough to eat, but this insignificant wife had even less. She was not allowed to sit at table with the rest of them but was banished to the kitchen. At table they all had to sit properly and not get up till the meal was over, but Hongying, being the youngest, was indulged by her parents. When she was quite little, she used to wander about during meals, carrying her bowl. She often went to the kitchen to give some of her food to this despised wife; she took her side as well, stopping her husband from hitting her. She learnt from early childhood to take the side of the oppressed, a principle which she followed all her life.

One day, this young woman was carrying a large bowl of hot food for the family's supper. Hongying was, as usual, running about and on this occasion collided with her. She dropped the bowl, which was smashed to pieces and the food spilt all over the ground - quite a disaster in a poor family. Er-Ge, who could fly into terrible rages, and nobody but Hongying could stop him, shouted that his wife was to

22

blame and ran to the kitchen for a knife. Hongying managed to calm him. "You are stupid," she said, "it was all my fault. Kill me if you want!" The unhappy woman never forgot that Hongying had saved her.

This second brother felt it his duty, according to Chinese custom, to produce a son - and to satisfy his mother. She had compelled him to go to his wife, whom he disliked so much, during her fertile period, and this resulted in a baby boy,Mingzhang, who grew up to be a doctor and teacher of anatomy. Another son, born several years later, was a lovely baby but died when he was only three or four. However, by now, Mingzhang was thriving, and Er-Ge felt free to leave home. He went to live in Singapore and changed his name from Liao to Qiu, his mother's maiden name, because his father-in-law had had no son to follow him. After some time, he became headmaster of a Chinese school there. Many years later, after Hongying had come to England he wrote and asked her whether she would approve of his marrying his secretary whom he had come to love. Before Liberation (in 1949), there was no possibility of divorce. Hongying objected that this would be bigamy, but she never heard whether they had in fact married. After her brother died, a parcel came to his son in Chengdu, containing letters, his watch, his fountain-pen etc. but those letters and photographs which would have told her more about his life are lacking. Nevertheless, she blamed herself ever after for having refused her consent to this happiness of his. Mingzhang, in May 1994, tried to persuade Hongying to stop blaming herself about it, but in vain.

As a conclusion to this story, when Hongying went back to China with her husband in 1959 for a visit, she saw Er-Ge's wife in Chengdu, and found her happy in being with her son and daughter-in-law - happy for the first time in her life she said. When Mingzhang's wife was expecting a baby, she sent for 'Granny', and they were contented in being together. In 1959 this baby boy was then four. He was allowed to come home from his Infant School to see his aunt. This woman who had been abandoned by her husband had found her happiness in caring for her grandchild.

To conclude the story of the marriages in Hongying's family, her third brother, San-Ge, married a tall nice woman. She and Hongying were devoted to one another, but her grief was that she didn't have any children. In old China it was thought a disgrace to be barren, and she was once found trying to hang herself in the kitchen. Da-Sao and Hongying cut her down. Afterwards, Hongying took her to school where she would be safe from her husband's reproaches, and found a matchmaker for her. The end of the story is happy: San-Sao married again, very contentedly and bore children and was content. San-Ge also remarried and had two sons and two daughters. Some of their many grandchildren are now, or have been at University. In fact, their eldest grandchild now teaches mathematics at the same school where her eldest brother used to teach.

Lastly, Hongying's sister. She married very young, little more than 15. Her husband's father was a rich landlord with two wives, and it was the concubine's son whom she married. He had been a student at her eldest brother's school - that quiet place in the Confucian temple where he used to teach. She had often seen him there when she was little, and he came to their house as well before his marriage. The sister used to hide herself on these occasions as bride and groom were not supposed to see each other before the wedding. Perhaps she had tried to peep through the window to see what her future husband looked like!

Because of their family's reputation as scholars, it was

an honour to marry a Liao bride. The bridegroom's mother used to send jewellery and gold for her sister's use. Although this mother was a concubine, she could read poetry; her husband taught her and she was obviously intelligent. She and Hongying became really fond of each other. This rich landlord's first wife also had a son and the family wanted this son to marry Hongying (though he would have been of a younger generation). Da-Ge was furious at the suggestion: "This precious sister, she's not going to marry anyone yet - she must study first and become a scholar."

Hill in Changting where Hongying used to walk with her second brother, Er-Ge. London Mission Buildings in the foreground.

Part 2. Schooldays.
Rumblings of Revolution.
1911 - 1927

Tentative beginnings

When she was about six, Hongying was thought too old to go on being taught at home and was taken to school - a private school in a former Catholic church. It was run by one of her father's friends, a Mr Wu, and consisted of about 20 boys and one girl of around Hongying's age, the teacher's daughter. One of the chief things she remembers about it was the banana trees in the garden and masses of plants with yellow flowers, possibly marigolds?

The schooling was conventional: the pupils had to learn the Confucian Classics by heart. First thing in the morning, the children would line up and be made to recite, standing with their backs to the teacher. If they couldn't remember something, they were punished. Hongying didn't like this place, especially the big rough boys; So after eight or nine months, she begged her father to let her stop going there. But in those few months, she had sampled all the *Four Books: The Great Learning, Doctrine of the Mean, The Sayings of Confucius* and *Mencius*, and could recite some pieces by heart, though of course at that age she didn't understand them - they were in a complicated classical form of Chinese.

The next stage in her education was to attend a missionary Sunday School. The daughter of a neighbour across the road who lived in a house with a filthy yard and a lot of pigsties, noticing her enquiring nature said "Won't you come to my Sunday School?" Hongying didn't know quite what this was but went all the same. They were told stories that didn't seem to make any sense to her - stories with pictures of bearded men and tall foreign women. After the stories they were given tea and biscuits. Hongying thought it was wonderful! They had milk in their tea - unlike the Chinese custom, and as for the biscuits - they rarely had anything sweet! She reported at home what a wonderful time she had had, but her father despised the foreign religion: "No foreign religion!" he said, "our Confucian teaching is the best in the world!" Her sister said it was shameful to like foreign food. Their mother said nothing.

A 'proper' school - moving towards western ideas

Hongying wanted so much to go to a missionary school - a 'proper' school, but it was said to be out of the question: it was foreign and it was connected with a strange religion. Her father would not hear of it at first. But she was a determined child and kept pestering him so much that after a year or two he gave in and let her go. Er-Ge brought her to school on the way to his own school in the hills. On rainy days he carried her on his back with the water pouring down on them both.

This was a school entirely for girls, or rather girls and women, for most of them were much older than her. Some were the servants of western missionaries, or the daughters of 'rice-Christians', that is Chinese who professed to accept the Christian teaching in order to get some material advantage (some rice to eat). Such was the poverty and the lengths to which people would go at that time. Others were wives or concubines of upper-class families. In the 'twenties some of these concubines had husbands who were studying in France or some other western country and who insisted that their

Schoolfriend of Hongying at primary school. Taken 1981.

women should study too, so they were of all ages. They looked on Hongying with admiration and said she was so clever, but she used to assure them, she was no cleverer than they were, only she had been taught at home since she was two and had had a sound start; she didn't need much effort to get the top marks. At her entrance, she had to pay one silver dollar as school fees for a year, but when, at the end-of-the-year exams, she came out top, she was exempted from paying anything more. That silver dollar was the only money that was ever paid by her family for her education!

When she was seven or eight, she remembers getting for a prize a doll with eyes that would open and close - *yang wa-wa* (foreign baby) Her family was entranced by this *yang wa-wa*! Everybody wanted to put the baby to sleep, even her brothers!

The subjects they learnt at this school were no longer confined to the Chinese Classics; they also had History, Geography, Arithmetic, Singing and Gymnastics - and of course Scripture. Hongying remembers a fat teacher called Mr Chang who told them in a sing-song voice about the sinking of the '*Titanic*'. It meant absolutely nothing to the children who had no idea of the ocean or of great ships, and could not imagine the tragedy.

They had a kindergarten teacher from Fuzhou or Xiamen called Lai. She had heard about Hongying's second brother, that he was such a learned person and questioned everything, so she gave Hongying a New Testament as a present for him. She duly took it home and gave it to him but he tore it to bits and threw it in the dustbin, and a second copy met the same fate. Hongying was convinced that Miss Lai was in love with him, but he was not likely to be attracted to her - like his father, he despised the foreign religion. Later, during the war against Japan, she married, but both she and her husband were hit by a bomb and were killed. Hongying had been really fond of her (although she had never been taught by her).

One of the class teachers was Liu Cifu, the wife of Fu Lianzhang, who later took part in the Communists' Long March. Fu, also from Changting, was trained in the mission hospital there and became Mao Zedong's doctor. He was persecuted and died during the Cultural Revolution, in the late 60s.

At the time, Hongying despised this Liu Cifu because she was always talking about boy friends, and some of the girls were not much better. Their classroom had a bay window facing the hills: those who sat by the window would watch the boys going by and giggle and exchange glances. Liu Cifu had an eye for them too.

As long as Hongying was at this primary school, she used to study at night in her parents' bedroom. It had the standard wedding furniture, but no chairs: there was just a high stool to sit on and a long desk with drawers and an oil lamp with a grass wick. If she was not studying, she only needed one wick, to give a dim glow, but for reading she had to have two or three. But then her mother would complain that it ate up too much vegetable oil. In Guiyang, during the Japanese war, she was reduced to a single candle to read by: she remembered her childhood and 'teens, and her one grass wick.

She had no pens, which were modern and expensive; the traditional writing instruments were brush, and an ink stick ground with water on an inkstone. To simplify matters, Er-Ge borrowed a slate for her. She always considered herself a clumsy person - dropped things like the slate-pencil for instance, but if she dropped the pencil, then she would have to climb down from her high stool. Her adoption of Er-Ge's philosophy of 'now or never' to do this tiresome thing, dates from that time.

One day, when her brother was out, she cracked the slate - the precious borrowed slate, and they didn't have enough money to buy a new one! It was a real disaster and Hongying was too shocked and frightened to confess, so she lied, saying it was like that when she first had it. Her brother sternly rebuked her: "You're telling a lie!" This was the first and last time that she lied to him.

As long as she was at primary school, she used to bring lunch with her évery day - just a bowl of rice, except after the New Year. Then the children would each bring some sticky rice cakes. These cakes were the traditional New Year food (as well as deep-fried *doufu,* a kind of bean-curd). Every family would fill a big earthenware jar with the cakes, pressed down tightly, with salt in between the layers to preserve them. In her family, they lasted about two months - two cakes for every lunch. At school, they put them in the big steamer to warm up.

In the last year of primary school, Hongying became a boarder. She was often ill at school, with colds and dysentery; the second time that her mother came out of doors was to visit her when she was ill. It was only a 15-minute walk; she made it slowly, being so unaccustomed to walking. As a Hakka woman, Hongying's mother's feet were not bound.

It was her missionary teacher, Marjorie Rainey, who wouldn't let her go on living at home because there was never enough to eat, and what there was didn't nourish her. Marjorie provided her with an egg every day, which she couldn't have had at home, and unpolished rice, for Vitamin B. She ate this special diet by herself daily. She hardly ever went home now, even in the holidays, because of this problem, but actually she much preferred to stay at school at this stage. It was clean and there was a cheerful atmosphere, whereas at home there was constant discord between mother and daughters-in-law. At that time, Hongying had despised women. Later on she realised that they were busy bringing up children and attending to all the minutiae of daily life: they had no chance to realise their own narrow-mindedness. At that point, she felt she had grown up; it was the social conditions that were to blame.

When she was at home, she was always hungry. She liked to be in the kitchen, to smell the cooking, and in the hope of getting some scraps to eat. But all she was allowed was the *guoba* the burnt rice sticking to the bottom of the pot. Again with her clumsiness, she tended to break bowls and dishes. So it was "Don't come into the kitchen!" She wasn't allowed to do anything there, hence what she later said was her inability to do much cooking, after she was married.

When her brothers were studying or teaching, and only came home at weekends, the elder one was given special food by his mother: steamed eggs with crystallised sugar. 'The elder son coming home' was a tradition in rural China. But her mother only kept chestnuts for Hongying when she came back - all she could afford (for a girl!)

There was a big well near her school. On those weekends when she stayed behind, she had to fetch water from this well and wash the school floors. They worked in teams of three and because she was doing well at her studies, she was her team leader. She had two 'Bible women' under her who did the actual cleaning, because, as they said, "You're no good at it!": She hadn't had any home training. They were peasant women who had learnt just enough to read the Bible and were content to do manual work; they would climb over the railing and stand on the very rim of the well - so courageous! she thought. Sometimes when they had gone in with the water, she would get another bucket and very gingerly try herself to pull some up. She brought up little fishes!

At her graduation from primary school, Hongying made a speech that was reported in the local press - probably the first time for a girl to come forward so boldly and so ably. She was only sad that her father was not there to see and hear her. He had died before she left primary school. There was only one other girl in this school, somewhat similar to Hongying. She was the daughter of one of the teachers and was one or two years older. Her name was Zhong Pinlian. The county gave money for one girl to study abroad, and Zhong got this first scholarship. She studied dentistry in Singapore and learnt music - the first educated woman from the county of Changting. Hongying was the second and by rights should also have had this scholarship, but when her turn came in 1927, the revolution had broken out and there was no money available.

Secondary school at Nanchang

Hongying was 14 when she finished at primary school. There was no secondary education for girls in her county and she was thought too young to be sent far away, so they kept her on at her old school as a class teacher. She took charge of the girls immediately below the top class and taught them all

32

Hongying in Changting c. 1924.

subjects except Gym and Music - for five years. Then she was deemed old enough to go away from home.

The normal thing would have been for her to be sent to Fuzhou, the provincial capital, but the dialect there was not understood anywhere else. Hongying was convinced that she didn't want to work in those conditions - she must go where *putonghua* (standard Chinese) was spoken, however inaccurately. So on the advice of the school principal, Marjorie Rainey, who saw how promising she was, it was decided that she should go to a missionary high school - run by the American Methodist Mission at Nanchang, capital of the neighbouring province of Jiangxi.

She went with a girl called Fu Weiyu, sister of Dr Fu Lianzhang. They set out in the winter vacation, around the New Year of 1923 - 24. They had one sedan chair between them, to rest in occasionally and to carry the little baggage they had. It took two days then to cross the mountains between the two provinces of Fujian and Jiangxi, through a Pass in the Wuyi range; then they embarked on a little boat on a tributary of the Gan river. The whole journey took two weeks. One can only imagine the mixed emotions of the two girls who had never before travelled beyond the quiet town of Changting.

Nanchang was in an area where Southern Mandarin was spoken, and most of the population still used the local dialect. Hongying remembers the shock of this discovery and how the two girls wept when they arrived because they couldn't make head or tail of it. To make matters worse, the cooking in that province was *la* (peppery) and they were not used to this. In school, Hongying found she didn't fit in with the other girls either, at first. The oldest pupil at that time was a girl called Yang Bing, the daughter of a rich family. With her silk clothes and leather shoes, she made a striking impression on Hongying who wore only coarse cloth and cotton shoes - a girl from the country. Because she had been teaching for so long, Hongying was much more advanced in mathematics and other subjects, but she was backward in English and had to sit with the Primary School children for this subject. From early childhood, she had learnt the Classics by heart - the *Odes*, the *Four Books* etc. Er-Ge had taught her day and night. Under his supervision, she had read some Chapters from the *Zuo Zhuan* (a history commentary) but more important for her future, she had learnt algebra from him. She was specially interested in mathematics, and for this subject she was allowed to work in one of the higher grades.

By the end of the first year at Nanchang, she had caught up with Yang Bing in all subjects and was in the same class with her; in the same dormitory too. This was a room with three beds occupied by Yang Bing from Hubei, a girl called Tan Huiying from Hunan, and she herself from Fujian.

Huiying, who was a Christian, had very high principles, was straightforward, and completely independent in her thinking. If she saw anything obviously unfair, she immediately spoke out. Once when someone had lost a special garment, the Head wanted to search everyone's case. Hongying protested, "You can search everyone's except Huiying's - she would never steal!" In fact Huiying was inquisitive; she did concern herself with other people's affairs, and that made her unpopular. Although they were so different in character, they soon became very good friends.

Yang Bing never talked much with the other girls on trivial matters; she was not one for gossip or small talk, but if she engaged someone in a higher class on political questions, she became really eloquent and drove her points home. Before she came to this school, her father had engaged a special tutor to teach her the Classics. She could recite long passages from the anthology *Gu Wen Guan Zhi* (History of Chinese Literature). She spoke well and logically. Hongying was the least eloquent of the three and, partly because she was not fluent in *putonghua*, she talked very little in the ordinary way. Her other schoolmates complained that she only spoke up at public meetings.

At night, in the dormitory, the three discussed everything under the sun. This was a wonderful time for Hongying: she was developing intellectually and learning about politics. Yang Bing talked about her autocratic father, who had already engaged her to be married. She didn't want to go through with the match - she wanted to be free, but her father was stubborn and severe. She was constantly thinking how to break free and often cried about it.

At that time, Hongying felt that Tan Huiying and Yang Bing were closer to one another than she was to either of them. For one thing, they were from neighbouring provinces, Hubei and Hunan, whereas she was very different: she came from the interior of Fujian and from a backward county, Changting, and she was of Hakka descent. The Hakka were the so-called 'guest-families' whose ancestors had moved there hundreds of years ago. (The people were too polite to call them 'invaders', which in fact they were.) The peasant women descendants of the Hakka in Fujian had, till recently, worn hairpins of silver, gold or bamboo in the form of swords or knives symbolically to protect themselves. They were denied the fertile land so that they had to live in the mountainous regions. They had very different customs from most northerners; for instance, their women never bound their feet. The leader of the Taipings, Hong Xiuquan, was a Hakka, as were many of his followers. It has often been remarked that the Hakka were stubbornly independent people.

However, most of Hongying's fellow students regarded the three of them as 'best friends'. The American Headmistress, Margaret Seeck, once told her that in her many years of work in education and long association with this school, she (and the other teachers there) had never seen three pupils who were not only not jealous of one another, but were such close friends as those three.

During her last two years at school, Hongying was responsible for ringing the bedtime bell, turning out the lights, and walking round the dormitories to see that everything was in order. Her health was never good and two or three days every month she would be confined to sick bay (the *kongqi fang* or fresh-air room) At these times, Yang Bing would do all these duties for her; she insisted that Hongying ought to go to bed early and not be given this responsibility.

One summer vacation, Yang Bing invited her to her home in Wuchang. They were a big family and Hongying was not used to their life-style, so completely different from that of her own family with its simple and regular routine. On that occasion, Bing's father and elder brothers were not at home - only the women and young children. It seemed to

36

Hongying that Bing's household had the 'Three Blessings' (*San Duo*): children, women and servants. The whole family didn't sit and eat together: they just ate at any time when they felt hungry. They told the servants when and what they wanted to eat. There's no doubt they were very rich.

The mother got up late. A servant would bring water for her to wash her face, then after breakfast, her personal servant would do her hair and help her to dress. By then, it was 2 or 3 in the afternoon. She would get into her private rickshaw and go to visit friends or neighbours to play mahjong. Then came lunch and a rest, and a visit to the opera with friends. In those days there was no special time for the opera to start: people came in and out as they liked, drank tea, ate melon seeds and sweetmeats. Everyone knew the opera stories, so it didn't matter at what point they arrived. Bing's mother came home at midnight and ate supper or dinner. The children's affairs were looked after by a woman servant - the mother didn't bother with them.

The revolution comes to Nanchang; arrival of the Northern Expedition

Meanwhile, on the larger stage, the general situation was growing more serious. 1926 was a time of sharpening struggle, when the young Chinese Communist Party had, on the instructions of the Comintern, joined forces in an uneasy alliance with the Nationalists. Their present objective was to unify the country, then being torn apart by rival warlords, particularly Wu Peifu and Zhang Zuolin; their instrument, the armies of the Northern Expedition which had been organised to move against the warlords from its base in Guangzhou (Canton). Not very much about the Communist movement filtered through to the small town of Changting, but Nanchang, where Hongying was studying, was another matter; it was very much the centre of the gathering forces. Hongying and her progressive companions couldn't help catching the excitement.

A pupil of Hongying's eldest brother, then at the Teachers' Normal University at Wuhan, wrote asking her to mobilise all those of her school who had forward-looking ideas about society, to go out into the streets and do propaganda. They were to tell people that the soldiers of the Northern Expedition were not like other soldiers, looting and carrying off whatever they could lay hands on. They were working for the people. They were going to oppose the levies and taxes of the warlords and to fight against them. These soldiers would soon be coming to Nanchang; people were not to be afraid of them.

In his letter, her brother's friend wrote that someone would soon be coming to Nanchang to contact her group of progressive girls (his name was not told her as this was underground work). Because the work was so secret, Hongying didn't know if anyone else in the school had had this letter - perhaps Tan Huiying or Yang Bing? In fact, those girls in the higher forms knew very well the purpose of the Northern Expedition, but not what they were expected to do to support the revolution. Besides, the missionary schools on the whole were opposed to violent change, and there were some members of staff who directly or indirectly supported the policy of their home government. Hongying's impression at the time was of the Principal's being sympathetic, but she couldn't be sure because there were other US teachers, sent by the missionary societies, who did not question their government's policy.

Hongying and her two companions, as leaders of the

Students' Union, represented their school. They went into the streets, marching and speaking at street corners, to explain to people the meaning of the revolution. They told the citizens of Nanchang who were puzzled and nervous about the situation, "These soldiers are fighting for you - to get rid of the warlords and corrupt officials" They hoped the townspeople would welcome their arrival, give them water and tea, carry their bundles and help the wounded to walk.

The girls in the upper forms now began to organise themselves into three groups to support the soldiers. One group was for nursing, one for sewing hospital clothes, making bandages and so on, and one for propaganda. Some went to nurse in the hospitals and some later married soldiers there. The three, Hongying, Tan Huiying and Yang Bing, all went into the propaganda group which they organised themselves. In Nanchang at this time, there was a wave of support for the revolution in all the middle schools and specialised schools, (there were no universities or colleges proper there at the time). The Communist Party sent representatives to organise them and the mission school couldn't stand against the tide. These were exciting times - to be young and part of a revolution!

Now, when they decided to participate in the students' movement in the city, they thought of cutting their hair short. To be considered 'radical', it was enough to have cut their hair in what was considered the Russian style; it was the sign of being revolutionary women. The question was, who would give the lead? It was quite a risky business! After the 1911 revolution against the Manchu Emperors, the men had cut off their 'queues' - the hated sign of Manchu domination. If the tide had changed and the Manchus had come back, these men would have lost their lives. Hongying decided she would cut off her hair and since nobody was bold enough to do it for her, she cut it off herself! (The older girls wore their hair in a coil or bun). Of course it was very rough and ready and looked pretty ugly. When the Headmistress heard of it, she asked her to apologise in front of the whole school and admit that she had made a mistake.

Hongying adored this Principal, a wonderful Maths teacher, but she refused to recant. She declared that short hair would prove to be the general trend and that soon the rest of the school would follow her lead. A few days later, Yang Bing cut hers. Then the two of them set up as barbers in a corner of the Hall and cut all the younger girls' hair.

In November 1926, the Northern Expedition arrived and occupied Nanchang. Hongying has some clear memories of it. She remembers the poet Guo Moruo - how handsome she thought him; and Soong Chingling, the widow of Sun Yatsen. As long as she lives she will not forget the emotions of that day!

Because they were now in contact with other Student Associations in the city, the mission schools, for the first time in history, started to have self governing unions (*zizhihui)* with the right to send representatives to any organisation. Hongying was elected Chairman, Yang Bing Chinese Secretary and Tan Huiying English Secretary. The three of them were now responsible for any activities connected with other groups in Nanchang.

Many questions were brought up for discussion. This took place in the large dining room, before or after a meal, and Hongying took the Chair. There was no Committee; all decisions were democratic. Tan's ideas were more Western and Christian. She emphasised self-cultivation and nobility of character. Yang Bing was very knowledgeable about the warlords: which areas they controlled, which were specially powerful, what they stood for. She understood their relative strength and their immoral and corrupt character. Their group read regularly the *Xiandai Pinglun* (Contemporary Review). From this, Hongying came gradually to understand international affairs and current trends. Later in life, she discovered how the US exploited the South American countries and oppressed them politically. She found out how Great Britain had robbed the Asian and African countries of their natural resources and politically dominated them.

On 12 April 1927 in Shanghai workers and young people were massacred in their thousands by armed gangsters working for the right-wing Chiang Kaishek. Out of fear for their safety, the Nanchang Students Association undertook no more large-scale organised activities.

Hongying and some of her classmates were busy preparing for their leaving exams. The schools had a special agreement with the missionary university of Yanjing; those who graduated with good marks could enter it directly without an entrance examination. Hongying would have qualified for this arrangement but since many young men from Changting, some of whom were her brother's pupils, were studying at Shanghai, Wuhan and Beijing and all were doing very well, she thought: "Though I'm only a girl, why shouldn't I join them?" She decided to apply to Beijing University, to study mathematics.

In June and July that year, the general situation became very unstable. It felt uneasy in Nanchang. Students frequently went on strike. To avoid trouble, the schools broke up early for the summer vacation; all the pupils were sent home as soon as possible. The final exams were not taken very seriously.

Leaving school and leaving China

Fu Weiyu and Hongying went back to Changting, leaving school in July. She planned to do some revision for the Beijing entrance examinations, but students coming back from Beida (Beijing University) reported that all the universities there were closed because the forces of the Northern Expedition would soon be arriving. They said they would not be going back for the time being.

Changting was a remote, backward county. The revolutionary waves had only just begun to rise there, but young people coming from other cities began to whip up feelings of revolt. Hongying joined their ranks, the only girl among them! This time, she was no longer speaking at street corners, as at Nanchang, but on the platform at mass rallies. A demonstration led by university students and young revolutionary officers once asked her as 'the best educated girl in the town', to speak at a mass meeting held in an open field. Not wanting to push herself forward, she refused at first but then remembered that Er-Ge had always told her not to be afraid of speaking up. So she made a long impassioned speech, not only discussing revolutionary problems but urging people to condemn any harm done to foreign residents in Changting as well, as injurious to the revolution.

Coming from a missionary school, she was conscious of the strong anti-foreign feeling that the revolutionary movement had turned up and vehemently declared the need to oppose it. She asked people to be considerate towards foreign residents in the town and condemned any harm done to them as uncultured from the national and racial point of view and injurious to the revolution. On coming down from the platform, she walked about among the thousands present, arm in arm with an English missionary. After this event, and a few more speeches, she was regarded as a local heroine.

"My point in telling you this" she explained in one of her letters to me later, "is that our revolution is not yet finished and it needs intelligent and fine leaders. It will go on for at least another 50 years." (letter 9.10.34) In this she was not mistaken.

Many years later, Hongying attended the Reunion organised by the Baldwin Alumna Program Committee for the graduates of 1919-56. (The school was called Baolin the Chinese version of Baldwin its American founder.) She noted then, "most of us are white-haired and nearly all of us are grandmothers," and added, as the briefest history of those years "those who graduated in the 1930s sang the School Song; another group of the 1940s sang the Song of Resistance; the graduates of the 1950s sang the Song of Liberation".

Former headmistress of Baldwin School

Hongying knew that her father had been a well-known figure in Changting, well respected and free of corruption. Her two eldest brothers were also highly thought of for their intellectual abilities. Her house was full of Award Certificates. The whole county knew their family. She felt she had a duty to be active, to make propaganda for revolution - why they had to get rid of feudalism, warlords and foreign imperialism. Chiang Kaishek, instead of opposing the invading Japanese, had turned against the Communists and left-wing progressives.

By now, Wang Jingwei had started to spread the White Terror in Wuhan. Special agents were active everywhere. They drew up black lists. Girls with short hair were looked on as Communist Party members and were persecuted. One of Hongying's primary school friends disappeared. Fear was growing in the county.

Hongying didn't realise her own danger, but her eldest brother as head of the family, was worried. He wanted her to go away for a time, but where was the money to come from? Marjorie Rainey then thought out a plan. She told Da-Ge, that she had funds in a London Bank and could send Hongying to England to live with her friends and learn English and then go to an English university. Was he willing for her to do this?

Her wise brother was delighted and grateful and urged her to go. Personal dangers, hardships and the hazards of a strange country did not count at all in his opinion. She should follow her education at all costs, in the country best suited to it. They both knew that Marjorie Rainey loved China; they believed that when Hongying finished at university, Marjorie would encourage her to come back to serve her country, and not stay abroad for good as so many students did. So she planned coming to England without any fear or suspicion.

There was no time to be lost. A few days later, her third brother took her to Hong Kong to catch the boat for England. On the way back he was captured by bandits and the family had to raise a lot of money to ransom him. Fujian being such a mountainous province, was full of bandits, more than other provinces.

Last stories of her schoolmates

To finish the story of her classmates, Tan Huiying and Yang Bing, with whom she had grown to womanhood and reached political maturity. After she came to England, she learnt that both they and another girl called He, all went to Changting and married Changting men. Her small backward town became a revolutionary centre; it lost 200 young men in the revolution. A few of her old friends wrote to her in England for a time, but she gradually lost touch with them. Letters from home always said, "Its a good thing you've gone away. We are having hard times here," and another time, "At your primary school, a Liao disappeared. Your brother-in-law and many other young people vanished without trace." This was in the years 1929, 1930. They were bad years; all these young people had been murdered by the Kuomintang. The news filled Hongying with sadness. Later on she learnt that Yang Bing had gone to Yanjing University in 1928. She was already writing articles under the name Yang Gang; she also wrote poetry. In fact she was fast becoming a professional writer.

For several years, apart from simple, brief family letters, Hongying heard no more from China. In British journals and newspapers, the articles about China only spoke about the extremist Nationalists (Kuomintang), warlord fights, banditry, high taxes, drought and floods, and how countless people lost their homes and went begging.

She had no news from any Changting people or schoolmates, except Yang Gang. In two successive years, autumn 1936 and Spring 1937, Yang came to Wuhan where Hongying was teaching after returning from England. She was carrying a baby, Guangdi, and looked ill and thin. Hongying asked her to get cod liver oil for the baby. The father, Zheng Kan, one of Hongying's brother's pupils with whom Yang Gang had been living, had been killed by a Japanese bomb. The next time they met was in Chongqing. Yang Gang was working for the newspaper *Da Gong Bao*, and Hongying went to see her in their offices. Her financial position was not good, she didn't even have enough warm clothes for the winter. Hongying didn't like long gowns, which women wore at that time; she preferred them shorter so as not to be hampered in walking. Since Yang Gang was not so tall, Hongying gave her some of her lined clothes. They met three times then, but they couldn't talk much as this was an area controlled by Chiang Kaishek. "Don't talk about national affairs!" was written up everywhere. At this time, with high prices and terrible inflation, it was a struggle just to stay alive. Many, sooner or later, left Chongqing. Yang Gang was sent to the US in the summer of 1944, as special correspondent of *Da Gong Bao*. Her daughter Zheng Guangdi, was brought up by the Communist Party.

In 1950, Hongying saw Yang for the last time. She was going to the Ministry of Foreign Affairs in Beijing, in a taxi when she saw her friend coming towards her, but they didn't speak. Seven years later, Yang Gang was in a car accident, also in Beijing. Even in the hospital she went on working. On 7 October 1957 she died.

Hongying felt she had lost a patriotic classmate and

friend, but also that China had lost a gifted poet and writer. Having worked for the Premier Zhou Enlai when he was also Foreign Minister, she had made an effective contribution to her country. In Hongying's eyes, she was a gifted and experienced revolutionary woman - someone rare in this world.

With Marjorie Rainey in England c.1931

Part 3. Escape to England. Learning English ways. 1927 - 1936

The great adventure

Hongying left China by P & O steamer at the end of August 1927, a journey of four and a half weeks, reaching London at the end of September. On board ship she naturally felt strange and lonely, but the idea that she was going to England, this unknown mysterious land whose people she could only picture from the English missionaries she had known in China, and was going to *study* - the great desire of her life - took the edge off her apprehension. But for someone who was by no means a seafarer and moreover had never been farther than the next province, those days and weeks must have tried her courage too.

It was still unbearably hot, especially in South China when she first went on board. She had just come home from school and had been hurried off with all possible speed for fear that Chiang Kaishek's secret agents would catch up with her. She was still wearing her school uniform, the summer one of black skirt and white cotton blouse. In her small trunk she had not brought nearly enough warm clothes: no padded gowns, only lined cotton, and of course no woollies. It wasn't possible to buy woollen clothes in China then, though there were Chinese orphan girls brought up by American missionaries, who had learnt to do all kinds of handwork. They could do cross-stitch embroidery, for instance, and many could knit vests and jumpers. But Hongying had never dreamt of attempting such work; her interests were in book

48

learning and politics. How did she survive at first in England, clothed from head to foot in cotton?

There were very few people travelling at that time because of the unsettled conditions in China and the consequent disturbance to trade and business, so she was given a first class cabin, - unbelievable luxury which she hardly knew how to cope with. She passed the long weeks in reading and playing deck games. Because her knowledge of spoken English was very incomplete, and not knowing what to say to most of the other passengers, who were making business trips, she didn't form any real friendships. One of the deck stewards took pity on her and became very attentive, but she in her innocence didn't realise that he might have other motives, and when one day he asked her, "Can I visit you tonight in your cabin?" she became frightened and locked her cabin door. From the next port of call, she sent an air letter to her missionary friend E. R. Hughes in Changting about this man. Hughes immediately cabled the P & O Company. He also wrote back to Hongying, saying that the steward had been discharged (he was not married), "So you are quite safe!"

E. R. Hughes had worked for the London Missionary Society in Changting, and was a lasting friend, adviser and support to Hongying, first in China and afterwards in England. In her early childhood, a highly respected Christian Chinese called Pastor Zhou had filled the post. He was the first Chinese pastor in her county and he it was who had said to Marjorie Rainey, "Watch that girl - she has a sense of fair play, and the courage to speak out!" In later years Hongying wrote to one of her Chinese friends about Pastor Zhou and his wife: "What I am is, in a very indirect way, due to their power of discernment." When Zhou retired his son-in-law took his place, but this young man had an affair with a primary school teacher who gave birth to a son looking just like him. So the Mission sent him away and wrote to the London headquarters about him. This was the occasion of the appointment of E. R. Hughes. Hongying was baptised by Hughes and she gradually became devoted to him because she recognised his great love and admiration for Chinese culture. He eventually left the London Missionary Society and devoted himself to the study of Chinese history. He asked Hongying to help him - he learnt Chinese from her and she English from him, a wonderful experience for her.

Arrival in England - first experiences

E R Hughes' sister Winifred (nicknamed 'Freddy') met her boat at Tilbury. Hongying was shy at first but soon found Freddy a very likeable person, warm and approachable. The Hughes' mother was still alive and lived with Freddy in suburban South Woodford, in a conventional middle-class home. That first night Hongying will never forget: she was so cold, she couldn't sleep all night. She kept wriggling about and finally got up to do some exercises. She was freezing!

Next day, Granny Hughes took her into Central London by bus. The old lady said she knew her way about London blindfold but in spite of this, they didn't really do much sightseeing, and after a few days of bewilderment, Freddy put her on the train to Bournemouth. There she was to live with two maiden ladies: Miss Brotchie and her aunt. Miss Brotchie was a friend of Marjorie Rainey, who had been a fellow-student of hers at Bedford College and had put Hongying into her care. That was how she came to stay with these two unmarried women.

Hongying told me long afterwards that one of the

things that struck her most about English women was that the minority who *chose* not to marry and have children were not full human beings. In China, very few women were unmarried, except those with very advanced ideas, who wanted a career, or who were protesting against the marriage system whereby boys and girls were betrothed to one another in childhood, through their parents' choice. And the idea of not wanting to have children was, in those days, utterly alien to Chinese thinking. Her view seems to have been rather extreme. She forgot that in the 1920s and 1930s, there was an imbalance of the sexes in Britain; one million (mostly young) men, had been killed in the First World War. So it was by no means always a matter of choice if women remained single.

Miss Brotchie's and her aunt's household was a very proper and genteel one, where they always changed for dinner, even if there were no guests expected. This seemed to be the custom in English middle-class families. Their house was always clean and neat and had plenty of china ornaments which seemed useless to Hongying. Her home had only the essentials.

Miss Brotchie herself was a delicate elderly lady. She looked after her aunt and did a little teaching of English and Scripture - both subjects were equally important in her eyes. Although she was quite clever, she never had a profession but lived on some private means. She went to Church twice every Sunday and to a prayer meeting on Wednesday evenings. Whatever she did she seemed to do out of duty. She had a sharp tongue, but basically she was a kind person whom fate had dealt a bad hand. No doubt she regretted not having married and probably resented not having achieved much in life, despite her talents, through being obliged to care for her aunt.

The going-to-church was a great problem for Hongying. In those days, all women were expected to cover their heads - their 'crowning glory' - in church. Miss Brotchie took her to a milliner's and bought her a hat with a brim. She had never worn anything like that in her life -she felt like a scarecrow! Then the serious side of the services, the up-and-down business as she called it - the kneeling and sitting and standing - this was so complicated, she simply couldn't follow it. Then she never could find the right place in the Prayer Book. And the priest in charge preached sermons which she could make no sense of. She remembers his jerky voice (the Reverend Mr Bostock) but has long forgotten everything he said. "Never mind!" said Miss Brotchie at the time; "he has a good Christian heart". For Hongying, he had no talent for reaching out to other people, and besides, his teaching had no intellectual quality.

Miss Brotchie cared very much for Hongying's Christian training. Day after day, she gave her lessons in the Bible because she hadn't come from a Christian family. As far as she had had Christian teaching at school in China, it was Congregationalist and Miss Brotchie was Church of England. She had to make a special plea to the vicar for Hongying to be allowed to attend.

In Bournemouth, she joined Chemistry classes at the local Municipal College. In 1928 she left for London, to take the Matriculation exam., at that time the first step to university entrance. She passed in Mathematics, Chemistry and Chinese (the classical language which she took instead of Greek or Latin), but failed in English Grammar. She decided to repeat the exam. and also to remain in London which she found much more intellectually stimulating than Bournemouth, a sleepy seaside town. She took a room in a King's College hostel and attended English classes at a special building in the Strand where students were prepared for Matric. Her teacher was a Mr Herbert Brinton, a retired master from Eton who had taught at this famous English public school for 40 years. She also learnt European History from a Dr Driver. What she chiefly remembers about Brinton was his advice to her, not to make a fair copy of the lecture notes: "if you copy everything, you'll never keep up" he warned her. She found this advice so sound that she followed it all through her studies.

The move to London helped her to grow up - to discover what she could truly believe. First she made contact with Harry Silcock who was Secretary to the Universities China Committee with an office in Gower Street. He had been appointed to look after the students sent to England by the Chinese government, the so-called Boxer scholars, very high-brow and standoffish. There were other students who were privately financed, and also some from Malaysia who couldn't speak *putonghua*. Hongying didn't feel comfortable with any of them. It seemed to her that for them, belonging to a group depended on social standing. She disapproved. She wanted to find out what was really important. This was not the first time that she felt isolated.

Harry Silcock was a Quaker and this proved crucial for Hongying. He took her at weekends to the countryside, to a country house in Buckinghamshire called Jordans. There were usually about 30 students there and she the only woman. On one occasion she asked to see a Quaker Church and experience their form of service. Great was her surprise to find the 'Church' was just a simple room and the 'service' merely a silence. There were no set prayers or hymns, no hierarchy, anybody could speak or pray, and especially no 'up-and-down', as she called it. In a very short time she realised, 'this is my place'. The quiet meeting suited her well;

53

she felt that the silence was more powerful than words and influenced people more deeply. Gradually she stopped going to any other Church; the 'up-and-down' had brought her to the Quakers.

At the end of the second year, she took English again, together with European History, but again failed the English. Then she was told, to her chagrin, that she had not taken the appropriate exam. This one was intended for students who were native speakers of English; there was a special syllabus for foreign school leavers. At this point she left London.

Approach to Somerville - support of Margery Fry

Hongying's aim was to study Maths at University. Her beloved Er-Ge had told her, "If you can master Maths, you can do anything", and she had heard that Cambridge had a high reputation in this subject. Besides, Marjorie Rainey, a Cambridge graduate, naturally assumed that this was where she would want to study. Accordingly she wrote there for particulars of the entrance requirements. However, when she learnt that at Cambridge women were awarded only titular degrees, not proper ones like men, she no longer wanted to go there. Here was a revolutionary young woman who believed in the equality of the sexes; what an insult for women to be denied a proper degree! She would try Oxford.

At Oxford she had no hesitation in selecting Somerville College. For one thing, the other women's colleges were named after saints - she didn't want to have anything to do with that! Then Somerville had a reputation for broadmindedness and welcomed students of all nationalities. When I came up in 1930, among my immediate friends were an Indian, a Russian, a South African and, of

54

course, Hongying, a Chinese - by no means a common situation in the women's colleges of those years. Then Somerville professed no particular faith. Where all the other colleges, for men and women, had their Chapels and supported the established religion, until the early 30s, Somerville had no similar building. Then, by a gift of one of its former students (the missionary Elizabeth Kemp), a somewhat faceless 'House of Prayer for all Peoples', in plain stone appeared to the west of the building called Maitland (dedicated on Jan. 19, 1935). Only a small proportion of students ever frequented it, but nevertheless we didn't consider ourselves 'heathen', but rather, 'searchers for truth', without the religious trappings. This appealed strongly to Hongying, both as the daughter of a Confucian household, and as a Quaker with a Quaker's lack of ceremony.

Another attraction was the fact that Somerville Hall (the forerunner of Somerville College, founded in 1879) had been named after a distinguished woman scientist and astronomer - Mary Somerville. So it seemed perfect for Hongying.

The Principal at that time (fifty years later) was Margery Fry. A strong supporter of women's rights who had once marched with the suffragettes, she had an unusual and lively interest in China. Hongying felt that she would be sympathetic to her as a Chinese and to her aims - she was also a mathematician, who, it was said, would turn to 'sums' in any slight illness as others would turn to light reading*. A few years later, in 1933, she was invited to China through the Universities China Committee, which was financed by a portion of the British 'Boxer Indemnity' (the compensation which the Manchu Imperial Government of China was forced to pay the foreign powers after its defeat in the Boxer Uprising of 1900). The scholars from both countries were

* See *Margery Fry, The Essential Amateur* by Enid Hwys Jones, OUP 1966, p.35

55

intended to learn about one another's cultures. Margery Fry was deeply impressed by China's art, the architecture, the philosophy and thought, as was her brother, Roger Fry the painter, with whom she was very close. (He was partly responsible for the widespread influence of Chinese and Japanese art on the work of the post-Impressionists).

Miss Fry was not at all like the intimidating idea Hongying had of a College Principal. She had a quick understanding and deep human sympathy. She looked at this outwardly diffident but inwardly determined Chinese girl, studying her with deep-set twinkling grey eyes, and Hongying felt she could talk with her about anything. Margery Fry had the inestimable gift of being able to put people at ease with themselves. When Hongying told her about having failed twice in English, her understanding interlocutor said, "I'm not going to bother you about English grammar (Hongying's bugbear). Just write me an essay on any subject you like".

All that time when she had been staying in Bournemouth with Miss Brotchie, she used to escape to London on any pretext. Her train always passed through Winchester, so she became familiar with the architecture of the very beautiful old Cathedral there. It touched her deeply and raised her spirits - there was nothing at all like it in China; she decided it should be the subject of her essay. Margery Fry accepted her without any further examination.

A fellow-student of ours, Enid Hwys Jones (Horton) in her biography of Margery Fry wrote that 'It began to be suspected by some of the sharp-witted and not always dedicated young women that the Principal was not wholly on the side of hard work, that those who got a Third in Honour Moderations were not necessarily in her eyes, as in those of the classics tutor, "lost souls"; Miss Fry certainly valued a

Somerville class of 1930. Hongying is seated third from right.
The author is thirteenth from left in the 4th row. Other college friends mentioned in the book are:
2nd row, 8th from right Joyce Brown, 13th Enid Horton, 15th Joan Blomfield
3rd row, 4th from right Rose-marie Hodgson, 6th Frances Newbegin
4th row, 1st from right Joan Browne, 4th Margaret Griffith
5th row, 4th from right Betty Horler.

young woman's human qualities more highly than academic brilliance.

The bond between principal and student continued to strengthen from that day; they never completely lost touch with one another, even through the war years. Hongying quite frequently stayed with her either in Radcliffe House, her beautiful home in a lane off the Woodstock Road, close beside College, or in her London flat where she later made room for Hongying and her English husband until they had a home of their own. She used jokingly to call Margery Fry, 'HF' (Heavy Father), a translation of the familiar Confucian term *Yan Fu*, Stern Father. Since Hongying's father had died, Miss Fry saw herself as the one who should morally guide her. "Miss Fry has been scolding me like anything (about not preparing her lectures). I call her Heavy Father. Well my Heavy Father says, she has never known anyone having so little sense of calendar". (Letter to I.H. March 29, 1936)

This is by the way. Having been accepted by the Principal, the next stage in her future studies was to take a general test in Maths. She was examined by the Senior Tutor, but couldn't pass the papers because in China she hadn't done first level Trigonometry, Solid Geometry or Calculus. The Tutor suggested she should study these first then apply again.

"How much longer should I need?" she asked.

"Three years", was the reply.

Hongying felt she couldn't wait. China needed her. The people were hungry...

She had heard of a famous Professor who lectured in Organic Chemistry - Robert Robinson. He had been seconded to an Australian University for two years and was now coming back to Oxford. Feeling that China's overwhelming need was for more food, she decided to concentrate on agricultural chemistry. But there was another obstacle here:

although English grammar was not required, she had to offer German, which she hadn't yet studied. She decided to take private lessons with a teacher of German in Oxford.

Picking up German

She stayed in Bevington Road with a family called Whale. John Whale was a distinguished Congregationalist Minister, and his wife was the daughter of another famous Congregationalist at Cambridge, Henry Carter. Marjorie Rainey as a fellow-Congregationalist, had asked the Whales to look after Hongying and let her lodge with them. Looking back, Hongying realises how very young and inexperienced she felt at that time.

She studied German with concentration for two months and gained a good knowledge of the grammar. In fact, her teacher said she was the best pupil she had ever had, but she had a hang-up about speaking, so it was decided she should go to Germany for the summer - to Freiburg in Breisgau, near the Swiss border.

Margery Fry had arranged for someone to meet her in Paris and accompany her to the train for Freiburg, but her shaky knowledge of spoken German landed her in trouble from the start. She couldn't understand the simple question, "Wohin gehen Sie?" (where are you going?) So in the crush at the ticket barrier, nobody told her the train didn't stop at Freiburg - or if they did, she didn't understand - so she was carried on to Basle (the train passed through Freiburg at midnight). She was quite scared and didn't know what to do. She had to stay in the station at Basle till the next train back in the morning. Luckily it was a warm summer night and the Stationmaster was very helpful, telling her she wouldn't come to any harm. "Just sleep on the bench" he said. "No one will disturb you." This was her introduction to Germany.

Her German teacher at Oxford had recommended this Freiburg Pension. It was run by a widow whom everybody called 'Tante' (Auntie) and was largely patronized by the lower-paid office workers who came in for their lunch. Among the guests was a German university student with his girl friend. Auntie was a good house-mother; she arranged for this student to coach Hongying, though as it turned out, he didn't help very much. He had no method and she studied mostly by herself, simply asking about passages she didn't understand. But in general she enjoyed Germany tremendously. The Germans, she found, were not, like the English, proud and stand-offish: they didn't have this "Don't touch me!" attitude to strangers. In a train, for instance, the English would hide behind their newspapers while the Germans readily made contact with the rest of the compartment, sharing their sausages and *butter-brot* and general bonhomie.

At the end of the summer, she came back to England, took the exam. in German, Classical Chinese and English Essay and passed easily. In October 1930, she entered Somerville - a great step forward after many set-backs which she had faced with her usual determination.

The Oxford student

The Oxford term always started on a Friday. The weekend would be spent - especially if one was a 'Fresher' - buying necessities, and mostly at Woolworth's for those who, like Hongying, had only a limited budget. Besides, the relative affluence of the Marks and Spencer era hadn't yet opened for any of us. Hongying bought a tea set (mugs had not yet become fashionable), cutlery, plates and glasses, and, at the Covered Market, various stores, such as cake, fruit and coffee.

She says she will never forget the first College dinner. The students queued to go upstairs into the big parquet-floored Hall with the dais for the Dons, the candelabras, the portraits in gilt frames of former Principals, including her heroine Mary Somerville, the Scouts (as the College servants were called) hurrying round to serve the food. In the queue, Hongying and I found ourselves next to each other (I had also come up that year to read English) and we began to talk. It was so simple to make friends in the easy-going, informal College atmosphere. I asked her to breakfast on Sunday in my room on the top floor of the building called 'East'.

This was one of the older buildings, not specially designed for a College, where most of the Freshers - apart from Scholars and Exhibitioners - were lodged. The rooms were quite small, but big enough for a friendly party, and furnished with bed, desk, armchair, bookcase, cupboard, and - joy of joys - a fireplace!. That morning, when Hongying arrived, she found me very excited. The novelty of having an open fire which one could light when one pleased! A symbol of privacy and independence. I had fried sausages on it and made toast by the red-hot coals on the end of a Woolworth's toasting fork, really costing only 6d in those days (Woolworth's prices were 1d, 2d, 3d and 6d). We could take bread and butter from Hall and make tea or coffee in one of the pantries to be found on each landing. This kind of meal was a revelation to Hongying: cooking in China was so elaborate even in a poor family. I had bought a teaset, I remember, with a dragon design - perhaps an omen for the interest in China which I was to develop later. We two have been friends ever since that morning.

In our second year, we could all put in a plea for the room of our fancy. Somerville was composed of a conglomeration of buildings, of different styles and periods, from Victorian with its curlicue gables to the absolutely plain institutional architecture of the 1920s. Such a building was the one called Penrose (after Emily Penrose, the Principal under whose eye the general design originated) at the Walton Street end of the garden. Built in 1927, it was rectangular, of grey-white stone and severely functional, but in the eyes of the 1930s undergrads, was distinctly 'modern'. It had a plethora of bathrooms, several pantries, and a students' laundry and drying-room, all excellently fitted-out - unbelievably convenient. So it is not surprising that Hongying should have plumped for Penrose and remained there for the rest of her time. She always put practical usefulness ahead of uncomfortable charm. My room in West (Victorian) was under the eaves, had interesting corners and charming windows, but the bathrooms in that building were few indeed.

College had plenty of social life, but not much of it appealed to Hongying. There was a formal Dance once a term, when we could invite young men undergraduates, but she said she could never make her feet move in that way, although many people tried to teach her. In Chinese cities such as Shanghai, the gilded youth were already practising the Foxtrot (and all the other dances), but this was not for Hongying. She disliked everything formal, such as changing in the evening for dinner. She couldn't bear to spend money on this sort of useless clothing. But Helen Darbishire, who succeeded Margery Fry as Principal in 1931 (Hongying's second year) was very particular about this custom. The stately procession of the Dons up to High Table in their

62

finery! We all trailed about in our long skirts. Hongying simply felt silly.

Because she was older than most of the undergraduates, Hongying was more interested in general ideas. There was so much that was new to her in the West - she could never have enough of discussion, over the dinner table or in rooms with our friends. She was often the last to leave Hall after meals. My picture of Hongying then is of her leaning over the dinner table, talking - or avidly listening - oblivious of the fact that the Hall was now practically empty. This was a wonderful time for everybody, a time for the free and broad exchange of ideas, but for Hongying it was a revelation.

She didn't pursue any sports or hobbies. She tried learning to swim and to play cards, but couldn't get on with either of them. The only game she had mastered (on the ship from China) was deck quoits. Later on, her studies became more demanding. She had lots of lab. work, and also walked a great deal with various groups of friends, her 'walking companions'. Chief among them were Joyce Brown (later, Holbourn), a quiet, clever girl who was First Scholar of our year, Marjorie Sorrel (Sidebotham), Marjorie Sale (Beastall) and Frances Newbigin. They gathered cowslips on Cumnor Hill, tramped together through Wytham Wood, visited the bluebells on Boar's Hill and wandered through the lovely Port Meadow with its grazing cattle and all the life of the river. On other occasions it was Joan Blomfield (Turville-Petre) later a Fellow of Somerville and author of many scholarly papers, and Enid Horton (Hwys Jones) who kept her company.

She also learnt to punt. She and five of her Somerville friends hired a punt for the whole summer term and we shared it between us, punting up and down the Cherwell,

63

often with a portable gramophone, wound up (as they were then) by a handle.

It was taken for granted that everyone studying at Oxford must have a bike, so Hongying bought a second-hand one; E R Hughes and his son David helped her learn to ride. Hughes had by then left China and been appointed Reader in Chinese at the University. Hongying remembers an event connected with punting and cycling that happened one May morning. It is a very old tradition - like much that takes place at Oxford - for the Magdalen College choristers to greet the dawn on the first of May with Latin madrigals. Hongying and a group of her friends had cycled over to this beautiful old building, listened to the songs floating over the park and river, then taken their breakfast out on the punt. Rose Marie Hodgson, one of the party (who later became a novelist and journalist) had brought a bottle of sherry in place of coffee, and this was our undoing. Hongying had never taken alcohol and did not realise that she was allergic to it, with the result that on the way home she fainted and fell off her bike. Another of our party, Betty Horler (later Rider, a teacher of mathematics) stayed too long on the end of the punt pole and fell in the river! (Somehow the story got about that it was Hongying, but this was not so).

Although there was so much about Oxford that engaged Hongying's thoughts - the human relationships, the widening of horizons, the intellectual challenges and the beauty of the surroundings - her College course gave her many problems. English secondary school students were accustomed to studying their specialized subjects to an advanced standard in the 5th and 6th forms, and had already done what she had to struggle with. Also a good number of Oxford students were from Public Schools: they had a kind of intellectual freedom which Hongying lacked and got on

64

quickly. Because of her different background, she felt she was lagging behind during her first year at University; in her Science Prelims, she failed twice in experimental Lab. work, which English students had already done at school. In fact, she felt out in the wilderness and was often quite unhappy about her lack of progress.

After finally passing her Science Prelims, she concentrated on Chemistry, but there was no Chemistry tutor in Somerville in those days; she had to go to Oriel College for tutorials, and there she had one tutor all the time, who provided no inspiration. They simply were not interested in one another (she still remembers his rather unpleasant voice.) She had to produce an essay every week but she never remembers his having commented on or praised a single one. In the Lab. work she had no guidance: she was just given a pile of cards with experiments written on them and she had to follow the instructions. She also went to Balliol College, which had a link with Somerville, for Spectroscopy, and for two years attended a course given by Professor Soddy on atomic transformations. This opened a new world to her.

Looking back, she feels she had no *teaching*. The opposite was the case in China: students were stuffed with teaching like Peking duck (force-fed); both methods ought to change. At Oxford, she said, students just attended lectures - if you didn't understand, you didn't understand and it was too bad. Also there were very few women studying Chemistry that year. Out of all the Chemistry students, only 7 were women: 1 at St. Hugh's, 1 at Lady Margaret Hall, 2 at St. Hilda's and 3 at Somerville. There were 90 men.

Oxford friendships

Because there was so little to inspire her in the teaching, she threw her energies and enthusiasm into Club activities, especially political ones. She joined the Labour Club, the October (Communist) Club, the United Nations Association, and also a Dancing group which met in the Quaker Meeting House. (It was through the Warden of this Meeting House that Hongying eventually joined the Quakers). Mary Trevelyan, a relative of the historian G. M. Trevelyan, conducted a choir for Folk Singing and Hongying joined this too. She had never sung before, except in Sunday School, at home in China, where they only sang hymns, but Mary was a good encouraging leader.

She had some political friends outside Somerville, one of whom was Percy Small (who was in fact very short) of Exeter College. He was a keen member of the Labour Party and quite often took her with him to meetings; they went walking together and she went back to his rooms for tea. Those were real teas, with crumpets toasted by the fire. He gave her a good understanding of the British Left, which was quite a force to be reckoned with in the Thirties. After the war, she wrote to him but got no reply; possibly he had been killed.

Another Oxford friend was Francois Lafitte. His father who was French and a Communist, lived in Hampstead. Francois took her to meetings of the Communist Club in Oxford and when she was in London, she used to go with him to a Chinese restaurant, run by a patriotic Hong Kong Chinese. She went to political meetings with him too; he was very well informed and wrote articles for the *New Statesman*. But eventually she was warned that their association ought to stop because her name was on the 'Black List' (kept by the

66

Chinese Embassy which had tabs on all the Chinese students in England). Hongying realised that she was still being pursued.

The comparative dullness of her academic work and the stimulus of the political meetings, especially for someone whose heart was set on social change, often made Hongying restless, even frustrated. The Chinese Communists were still struggling, but the Soviet Union seemed to grow in importance and was becoming a new world force. So when she had been studying for almost three years, on a sudden impulse, she went to Helen Darbishire, her Principal after the resignation of Margery Fry, and told her she wanted to leave College and go to Russia. "I want to work in Soviet Russia and make a new career there," she insisted.

Miss Darbishire, (known affectionately in College as 'the Darb') though very different in character from Miss Fry, with a shyness that covered a real understanding of the human beings in her charge, and a warmth that only communicated itself to those who knew her well, responded sensitively. She advised her to consult the Master of Balliol, Lord Lindsay, "for he is a wise person and very knowledgeable about those countries".

Lindsay was also sympathetic but he insisted, "Your interest is in China. China is a great country; your future and your country's belong to each other." From that time on, whenever she had a political problem, she would go to him.

I was one of Hongying's special friends at Oxford; another was Joyce Brown. She spent several holidays with Joyce and stayed with her family in Golders Green. She also stayed with my family in Bournemouth. Mine was another rather proper middle-class home, like Miss Brotchie's, with the difference that my mother was a gentle warm-hearted Scottish lady. She really cared for Hongying. My father had died when I was a baby, but Hongying found the home a happy one, especially in summer when it was full of young people - my friends and my elder sister's.

We three, Joyce, Hongying and I, had a wonderful summer vacation together in the Lake District, where we walked from morning till evening every day. We stayed at a farm in Little Braithwaite, not far from Keswick, and bathed in the early mornings in a cold stream that flowed from the foothills of Skiddaw. Hongying remembers the piano in the parlour on which Joyce and I tried to play Beethoven's Moonlight Sonata, I the slow movement and Joyce the more difficult fast one.

Frances Newbigin was another early riser. She used to swim in the Cherwell before breakfast in the Summer term. Hongying tried joining her but found the river bed too muddy: because she couldn't swim, her feet sank into the thick mud. She also spent vacations with the Newbigin family at a cottage in Morpeth, Northumberland. They were very much open-air people and went in for picnics in a big way. They would light a bonfire from rough grass, even when it was raining, and brew tea. Hongying couldn't light such a bonfire - the Chinese rarely had picnics then - and the failure made her miserable. Frances' brother was much involved with the Student Christian Movement and later became a leader in the United Church of South India. Frances' faith was of another sort: she joined the Oxford group (afterwards called Buchmanites, after their American founder Frank Buchman). Hongying tells the story of how the College Secretary of the United Nations Association, on going round for contributions, came to Frances Newbigin: "Wait till the evening" said Frances, "and I'll ask God". Hongying felt like protesting, "God has given you intelligence; can't you even decide about a penny?"

68

Getting ready to go home

In 1934 Hongying took her Chemistry Finals and joined the School of Agriculture to get a B.Sc. She now studied under a Professor Watson, working in the lab. on soil analysis, but this again proved dull and monotonous because she worked on only one soil - from the Sudan. She thought she should have been comparing different soils, and this caused her lively disappointment. There was no direction and the Head of Department was a commonplace person - just as in Oriel. Perhaps there was a prejudice against Chinese, as well as against women? Churchill had said, "What's China? A yellow blob on the map!" This was then the general attitude.

There are negative factors in our own feelings and make-up, she thought, looking back long afterwards. If she had had good teaching, she might have become a good chemist. If she had overlooked the slight to women at Cambridge in not awarding them full degrees, she might have found the Science Course there much more fulfilling.

She got her B.Sc. in the summer of 1935. That year, at Margery Fry's house, where she was staying for the vacation, she met the famous Chinese geologist, Li Siguang (James Lee). He asked her if she would like to go to Wuhan University. Her reaction was that she needed to do more research - to specialize in agricultural chemistry, but the idea interested her and seemed a hopeful opening. Wuhan was just starting a new Department of Agriculture and she would be in charge of Soil Analysis. In the event, Li Siguang persuaded Wuhan to give her a year's salary so that she could continue to qualify herself in England.

With this money, Miss Darbishire arranged for her further studies. She went first to University College, London, to do Lab. work in analysing food - applying Chemistry to practical analysis. Then she went to Aberystwyth to learn about dairy produce and the different grasses. Bangor was famous for experiments with grass - what was best for cows and sheep. She also studied at a Horticultural Station, learning how to grow, cut and pack flowers and keep them fresh for market. Lastly she went to the Rothamsted Experimental Station, the world famous research institute, to do field work.

This was a very fruitful period: practical experience through Helen Darbishire's advice; she felt as though she were coming to grips with the real problems of the real world. While in London, she also attended lectures in Statistics at Imperial College, given by Hyman Levy: how to plan experiments, collect samples, and how to calculate (random sampling for statistical analysis). Levy had a great influence on her, she used to claim. Besides being an excellent mathematician, he was on the Left in politics and showed her the social relevance of what he was teaching.

In the Easter vacation 1936, Miss Darbishire arranged for her to go to Glasgow. Up till then, she had seen very little outside Oxford and London, and even there, it was mainly the University world that she experienced. Miss Darbishire didn't want her to go back to China thinking that all of Britain was like Oxford. Every morning she worked with a Social Services organisation, visiting the homes of poor people in Glasgow and interviewing those who needed help. Glasgow shocked her deeply: the filthy doorways with faeces and spilt beer on the steps, the poor women in dirty, ragged clothes who came for financial support. She was supposed to talk to them and find out about their situation but she had no idea how to do this social work - didn't know what questions to ask. She kept looking at the clock to see if it was time to go back to her digs. She didn't think she was at all fitted for such work.

While in Glasgow, she indulged her favourite occupation of walking, travelling with a group of Scots people into the wilds of Inverness-shire. They climbed Ben Nevis! What a joy this must have been for her. She had always loved mountains - more than water, of which she was secretly afraid. But the mountains of her homeland - how the memory of them moved her!

She made friends in Glasgow with a woman called Isabel who later married Hugh Douglas, a Scottish Minister with a church in Dundee. They wrote to each other for years, until interrupted by the war in China. She had another friend, Isabel Waller, whose father was Italian, a manufacturer in Manchester and very rich. (She had studied at Cambridge and came to know Marjorie Rainey through the Carters). This Isabel was rich too, and very generous - in the real sense, not a philanthropist for her own glory. "No money - no matter!" she would say. Marjorie had written to ask her help with Hongying's general expenses and she contributed whatever was needed without a question. With this money, Hongying allowed herself certain 'extravagances' such as going to concerts. Isabel married Colin Waller, quite a poor man, who became lecturer in English at Manchester Unversity. They lived in a big untidy house where goats and rabbits ran about freely. She liked the simple life, and also the primitive crafts. She would spin wool for instance. Hongying found her open-hearted and genuinely good and she loved people. There was a wonderfully free atmosphere in her home.

In the summer of 1936, Hongying was ready to return to China. She had her degrees and research experience. She also had with her a portable gramophone and the records of several Beethoven and Mozart symphonies, the gift of Margery Fry. Many people had asked her, "why don't you stay in Oxford and do some more research?" She always replied, "Because China is a vast country and there are natural calamities almost every year. The people need food, so I must help to improve the agriculture." Her heart was dedicated to China, not to self-improvement.

One of her Oxford friends, Joan Browne (Principal of Coventry Teachers' Training College among other posts) told me how impressed she was at Hongying's having chosen a subject - Agricultural Chemistry - in order to help her country. Most of us read what satisfied our heart's desires - or might lead to a 'good job'. Not so Hongying. Her high school music teacher at Nanchang had encouraged her to specialise in music, for which she undoubtedly had a gift. She learned to play the piano to quite a high standard, and took part in the concerts which the School gave every term to parents and local dignitaries. She also played the harmonium to accompany the younger children's physical training. But Hongying wouldn't hear of such self-indulgence as studying music for a career: what relevance did it have for the sort of world in which she was growing up? However, music stayed with her all her life: one of her great pleasures is in listening to choral singing and orchestral playing, and watching players and conductor. She is especially fond of the organ - perhaps a throw-back to the harmonium she played in the primary school?

In her last year at Oxford, Joan Browne looked over the English of her thesis. Together with Ann Wolfe (Humbert Wolfe's daughter) who harboured them in her room, the three of them talked a lot about the state of the world and what their part in it might be. In poetic mood she wrote to me before she left England, "I'm glad to have chosen this line for my profession. It deals with growth, life and that is beauty itself." (June 1936)

From time to time, she was overwhelmed by China's

sufferings, by the enormity of the task she was facing. On receiving news of her brother's illness in Singapore, she wrote to me (30 November 1933): "It is not only my family, not only any particular illness. It is something deeper and of a general nature: the whole population of the country is suffering. We are so poor, so much underfed, and so none are well and strong. I seem to be the only one, greedy and surviving like a weed. No one is to be blamed. The problem is far too deep .... it is a problem in history."

Map showing places mentioned in the text

73

Part 4. Return to China.
War and marriage.1936 - 1944

In the summer of 1936, Hongying was travelling back to China - a very different person from the shy high school graduate who had sailed for England nine years before. She had left behind many friends and a way of life that had become, in part, familiar, and she was to teach at the National Wuhan University, a new venture in Chinese education and at a critical point in China's history, one year before the outbreak of hostilities with Japan.

In Europe as well as in China, the world situation was becoming increasingly tense and fragile. "Europe smells of war", she wrote to me from England in January 1936. "This evening I listened to news broadcasting for the first time after a very long period and it was full of war air", and a month later, "In Europe, it is very bad. Talk of armaments is everywhere and all the time, without any exaggeration. Miss Fry constantly listens to News and says "Ghastly!" I feel too depressed to listen any more. It appears something will happen during this year, both in Europe and in Asia"...

Meeting her nephew Mingzhang and exploring some beauty spots

She boarded the ship at Genoa on 31 July - the S/S Conte Verde of the Lloyd-Trestino Line. On the long journey by sea from England, they put in at Singapore, where her beloved Er-Ge was teaching. He met her and brought her to meet his friends; the joy of this reunion can only be imagined. This brother had been responsible for her

74

upbringing and now he was asking her to take charge of his only son, Mingzhang, and supervise his education "because I can't trust that woman" (his mother). So when Hongying embarked once more and arrived at Hong Kong, the young boy, then about 14, was brought to meet her.

Mingzhang, accompanied by his mother, had reached Hong Kong by a devious route. In 1933, when he was 11, she had taken him on foot to Shanghang, a town not far from Changting, where San-Ge (Hongying's third brother) was living at that time. He installed mother and son in the house of a paper merchant. Shanghang was a paper-making and exporting area. They stayed there till the end of the year, then spent the Spring Festival of 1934 in Chaozhou. From Shanghang to Chaozhou they had sailed in a small wooden boat which transported paper on the lower reaches of the Ting River, across the border from Fujian to Guangdong. They took a small motor-boat to Dapu and a larger one to Chaozhou. (Their expenses, about the equivalent of 20 Silver dollars, were paid by San-Ge out of Mingzhang's mother's money.)

The day they got to Chaozhou, he installed them in lodgings of doubtful reputation. Next morning, San-Ge went to see the father of his cousin Li Hongdong, who as soon as they started discussing the situation, wanted Mingzhang and his mother to move into his house. So they moved in and lived there until 1936.

How Mingzhang and his mother came to Hong Kong to meet Hongying's boat was also connected with the Li family. Hongdong, while at middle school in Changzhou, developed TB. At that time, there were no facilities there for treating this disease, so he went to Hong Kong in 1935. Half a year later, his mother went to visit him and on that occasion, took Mingzhang and his mother with her.

When Hongying first met Mingzhang in Hong Kong, she found quite a tall boy with a shock of upstanding hair (which she was always trying to tame). He was thoroughly bewildered by the big city, the big ship, and his clever aunt in her English clothes. The two of them travelled on to Shanghai where I was waiting to greet her on the docks. During the year when she had been doing her practical research, I had been studying classical Chinese at the School of Oriental Studies with the intention of becoming a translator of Chinese classical literature. I had come to China ahead of her, stayed in Ginling Women's College through the Winter and Spring of 1936, and had been receiving tuition in poetry and calligraphy at Nanjing University. We were going together to Wuhan University (Wuda) on the upper Yangzi, where Hongying had been appointed lecturer.

Term had not yet started so we decided to explore some of the beauty spots in the neighbourhood of Shanghai. We went by train to Hangzhou, Suzhou and Taihu, the huge lake between Jiangsu and Zhejiang province. Always one to be attracted by the practical side, Hongying was specially interested in the irrigation works on Taihu and went over the whole process with the Director. At Hangzhou we enjoyed the local shrimps and tea (the famous Dragon Well) and went boating on the beautiful West Lake and admired the willows all along the edge. In August the days were terribly hot and damp; most of our exploration took place in the late afternoon. We climbed the hills, walked in the still bamboo forest and paddled in the Valley of Nine Streams and Eighteen Brooks. It was at Hangzhou that we were joined by Henry MacAleavy, the 'brilliant mischievous scholar', as one of his friends described him. During the War of Resistance to Japan, he worked in Chongqing and later wrote books on Chinese history.

His home was in Bournemouth; he had met Hongying there during her visits to Miss Brotchie, got to know her, developed a passionate attachment and wanted to marry her. But she had no interest in marriage at that time. Looking back over her correspondence, it seems to me that, despite her strong determination to serve her country, to the exclusion of all else, the gentler, more sensitive side of her character which appreciated art and poetry and especially perhaps music, made her susceptible from time to time to tender feelings - caused her 'to fall in love', as it is called. She fought against this strange sensation, and rejected the idea of marriage, for many years. When halfway through her College career she told me of her love for a German, she protested, "marriage is out of the question. I am born to do something else - home life makes me shudder and disgusted." This protest comes up again and again. Time and other circumstances changed her views on marriage, but never her dislike of the household chores that went with it.

As another comment on this subject, she had written to me in January 1936 about the young Chinese in London who kept pestering her. "My only answer to their play is my going to my job - as to my wedding. I really regard my going to Wuhan as to my husband! A feeling of security and happiness attaches to this coming event".

At Wuhan University; work and life

She had previously seen very little of her native land, and Mingzhang even less. He was very much in awe of his aunt and her English friend and hardly dared open his mouth. But the wonders of modern technology amazed him; he never ceased to be surprised and pleased by the running water in

77

the hotel where we stayed, and as for the WC, he kept pulling the plug and watching the gush of water with astonishment!

After a few weeks' happy wandering, we finally arrived at Hankou and took the ferry across the Yangzi river; there was no bridge over the river then - that was to be built later under the Communists. Wuhan was a comparatively new University, only eight years old at the time and still in the process of development. It had a lovely campus among the hills and lakes of beautiful clear water, and was far removed from the traffic of the neighbouring town of Wuchang. Because the whole area was so little developed, if one stood on one of the many hills, it seemed that the whole of China, plains and mountains, and behind them the rest of Asia, was stretching out to infinity.

The University already had Colleges of Arts, Law and Engineering, white buildings with brilliant green curving roofs, but the College of Agriculture was still unfinished; labs were being designed and equipment ordered, and the house which Hongying had been promised was unfinished as well. We were deposited at the Guest House for the time being. This was the first of the many frustrations that Hongying met with here and it quite blunted the edge of her enthusiasm. 'Periodically, I think the whole of that University is dead, dead as Ash (with a capital 'A')'. She wrote in one of her letters.

The Head of her Department was a Cantonese, experienced in Forestry and Agronomy; Hongying worked under him as an agricultural chemist. The best she could say of him was that he was a 'mean man'. He had been trained at Cornell and consequently favoured the US and US research; he was a pompous person, very anti-British, who had an Alsatian dog - a symbol of being Westernized. He was doing

78

research on maize; the new strain he bred was named after his son.

Hongying became quite friendly with a specialist in cotton-growing (at Liberation he became a Vice-Minister of Agriculture). His wife's sister was one of her students, which brought them closer. The Head of the College was a specialist in cattle and dairy-farming. The whole group, all US trained, worked quite well together, apart from the Head of Department.

Some weeks after we arrived, we moved into our new house. Hongying and I were to share it with an Austrian woman lecturer called Edith Czech Reschensky. She proved to be a quiet melancholy soul who left only a shadowy mark on our lives. (But she disapproved of our male visitors!) All teaching staff quarters were of grey stone and quite featureless. The high and mighty, the President, the Deans of Departments and other important persons had houses on a grassy hill (*Lujia Shan*), but we were on the plain below, not far from the lake. I used to swim there till November. We had a little uncultivated garden, but all around was wild marsh. In October, it was quite pleasant, but in winter the rooms were dreadfully cold, though we had a big iron stove in the dining room (which frequently went out) and I bought a small charcoal brazier for my room. We used to warm the wine by it, in the Chinese fashion, when we gave parties for the students. The back door, which led out of the dining room into the wasteland, was full of cracks, which we papered over with sheets of the *Illustrated London News*. We each had a room with a good solid desk, but in general, the furnishing was minimal. I don't remember much in the dining room beyond a table and chairs.

All our needs were met by a Chinese servant (*Dashifu*), who was a good, intelligent person, thrifty and sweet-tempered. He cleaned, shopped, cooked and washed up, carted coals and lit fires, carried messages and posted our letters, and his wife came once a week to collect our washing. Edith was always washing her underwear and cleaning her shoes. She complained that China was so dusty. Hongying supervised the menage to some extent, but since none of us was very interested in meals or housekeeping, we tended to leave it all to our capable servant. I only remember Hongying asking him to cook more vegetables - she was already moving over to the vegetarian side.

At intervals, we made expeditions to Hankou. Hongying always carried a neat canvas bag. After buying our various necessities: saucepans, chopsticks, nails and hooks, knives and spoons and so on, we treated ourselves to a meal at one of the many restaurants (we favoured the Cantonese one. We ate such delicacies as venison soup and a cake made of dates). We also visited a Japanese restaurant where we sat cross-legged on the floor and were served by attentive Japanese girls in kimonos.

Because we were such an isolated community, we had to make our own diversions. These were mostly dinner parties among ourselves. I remember a party in October when we had crabs and wine, the special food beloved of poets. It had been arranged by Ling Suhua (wife of Professor Chen, Dean of the Arts Department), a painter, calligraphist and a leading woman novelist and writer of short stories in the modern style. She was also a great charmer! I also remember a picnic on a small rocky island in the lake, on the Mid-autumn festival, when "the sky is the clearest and the moon is full and brightest in the mid-autumn sky, the clearest in the whole year" as Hongying described it. We ate the prescribed moon cake, and some of us slipped into the water to swim in that brilliance. Life with Hongying was something very special. She was the sort of person who made the most ordinary events of daily life more interesting because of her zest and quick observation.

Rather apart from the academic circle was Julian Bell, the writer and poet (son of Vanessa and Clive Bell and nephew of Virginia Woolf). He had been appointed to Wuhan as visiting Professor of English and Hongying and I spent many a lively evening with him at his house on *Lujia Shan*, agreeably furnished in the Chinese style and decorated with paintings by his family. We talked of everything under the sun, from Communism to the French Symbolists. We also invited him to our humbler home and played for him records of Mozart on Hongying's portable gramophone. I can still remember the expression on his face when the stylus touched the record and that ravishing music flowed out - an almost physical reaction.

Around Christmas time, Hongying and I collapsed with a bad attack of 'flu, and I incomprehensibly developed chickenpox as well. Julian packed us up and escorted us across the river to a small hospital in Hankou, run by Italian nuns, who cared for us beautifully and brought us presents of sweets, cakes and oranges on Christmas morning and restored us to health.

But although she and I had fun together, Hongying didn't really like the University life at Wuhan. She wasn't fitted for it. There was no sophistication, no urban life in that part of China then, and this together with her Oxford training meant that she didn't mix well with the rest, who were almost entirely US-returned students. In addition, there were very few women among the staff. She remembers one Chinese woman scholar, but she was much senior in position; she had established a name for herself as an academic writer - there was too big a gap between them academically. There was also a Miss Wu, a biochemist, very American in outlook and sympathy. To tell the truth, Hongying felt a bit too proud, and thought she had begun to lose her Chinese-ness. In our social activities, visiting the homes of the other faculty members, a lot of local gossip went the rounds. Hongying kept feeling that other members of staff were spying on her. It was all too narrow. After I had gone back to England, she complained bitterly to me about this persecution, as she called it. "Today a good colleague of mine told me that they all had heard in the Agricultural College: I am in love and there are two men trying to marry me. How these people persecute me, an unmarried woman! Three goodly ladies try to say something to me, which in effect amounts to this: they are trying to *introduce* me to someone to save me from further troubles. Introducing is the usual practice in marriage in this modern China, as if I would be a cow or dove."

Perhaps because the Agricultural School had not been established when Hongying arrived at Wuhan, the staff was given a project by the Beijing-Hankou railway. The University had been commissioned to look after the forestry and crops along the line, so the whole agricultural staff set out to investigate the conditions all the way to Beijing, sleeping on the train. Hongying was put in charge of the soil sampling. It was an exciting project and one that appealed particularly to her and she enjoyed the whole set-up. She wrote to me in November 1936 while on this expedition, "I really hate home life, in whatever shape it takes. I am born a vagabond and irresponsible. I love to be clean cut off from (it), to live a community one, whether in a College or a hostel or a hotel. Even the life in this dirty train is better than our Nunnery" (this is what we called our house with its three female occupants).

However, the labour was all in vain. War broke out

(the War of Resistance to Japan) the following July, the members of the group scattered and the whole investigation came to nothing. All the soil samples were lost in the Japanese bombing.

War and the trek to the West

On 7 July 1937 came the incident at Marco Polo Bridge (*Lugouqiao*). The Japanese occupied Beijing and Tianjin without a fight and were advancing on Shanghai. I had already gone back to England in March. My mother was ill and the approaching war in China and the feeling that the Civil War in Spain was of wider concern, made study almost impossible. Julian, on his return from an expedition to the borders of Tibet the previous summer, had heard of the outbreak of the Spanish Civil War. He too had now gone home and joined the Spanish Medical Aid. He was killed in July 1937 while on stretcher duty.

Hongying felt unspeakably sad and lonely. Japanese bombers came over. They had bombed Nankai and Central University; also Hongying's old school at Nanchang. The district was crowded with refugees, including over 2000 students. Food prices were soaring and some food coming to an end. The University was hardly functioning; they were learning nursing and making first-aid outfits. On 23 November 1937, Hongying sent a 'round letter' to her friends in England. "This is only to tell you that so far we are alive in the Univ. Events are taking place rapidly and the atmosphere is intense beyond description. We may break up any day, and then goodness knows where many of us (I am one of these) will go and do what. Men at least can go to the Front to have a struggle before dying. Women have nothing to do. No organisations to take our service if any. You see, we are not prepared for this war. It has been forced on us. I have no mind for writing letters. But you will be glad to know, I try very hard to work with the students in order to keep them a little more calm.

Do any of you know about hunting? I do not, but I imagine we are now like the hunted animals, innocent and stupid and now struggling for life or death."

On 3 December, she wrote to me again, in despair: "It is almost a complete anarchy here. People are really in a panic. Many families are gone or going soon and students too. I can't tell you the numerous stories of people dying while they are trying to escape from danger, or people losing family members or children on the journeys. Let alone luggage. There is no hope of carrying one's possessions anywhere...So I have been looking through letters and papers, and have thrown away *most* of them. I rather destroy them myself. I am waiting here till the last moment when the Univ. either officially breaks (up) or moves. No word to describe my state of mind, except agony to see one's country treated in such a manner and the worst agony is, to my mind, as you can guess by knowing my opinions of the Chinese, all the blame is on us ourselves. All our own fault to have made such a weak and sick country."

The Chinese Universities had already been ordered to move to the West. Wuhan had left its campus after the fall of Shanghai in November, when the Japanese were approaching Nanjing. Everything had already been packed up and those with families, the majority, had left in early autumn, August and September. Hongying, who had no family with her except Mingzhang, was one of the last to leave, at the very end of the year. All her belongings that she had saved: clothes, papers, teaching material and her current research, which had been loaded on to a river boat, were bombed by the Japanese and she lost everything.

She set off up the Xiang River in her summer clothes since her winter ones had gone to the bottom. Some young members of staff were in the same predicament; they carried their bedding rolls on their backs like tortoises. But they ran into bandits who stole their bedding and their overcoats. They stayed one night in Changsha, then walked to a village where they slept on the floor in the railway station, close together to keep warm, and with men on the outer ring in case of undesirable intruders. There were masses of refugees everywhere. On the border between Hunan and Guizhou provinces, they stopped at an inn. The police wanted to examine their papers but they couldn't read the University document. "Where's your husband?" they asked - couldn't believe she was unmarried. "I'm on the Wuhan University staff", she protested, "I shall go back there when the war's over", but it was no use. Finally she showed them her University identification badge and with this they were satisfied: "All right! You go!"

Eventually, after a very slow journey, they reached Guiyang. Hongying and Mingzhang spent the New Year of 1938 there with the Zheng family who had been travelling with them. Mr Zheng had been her elder brother's classmate. A Kuomintang appointee, he was now working for Dai Li, Head of Chiang Kaishek's Secret Service. They also came from Changting, so although they hadn't known each other there, this was an immediate passport to friendship. Zheng arranged for Hongying and Mingzhang to stay in the large house of another Mr Li, a member of the local gentry; he himself was Secretary-General in the provincial government.

The Zhengs were a friendly family and all got on well together. The only trouble was, Mrs Zheng took on all the shopping and used to appropriate some of Hongying's groceries - although they were not short of money. Her sons complained! She used to nip things out of other people's shopping baskets - maybe a kind of compulsion brought on by the war.

Guiyang was a backward place and very dirty, and there was a nauseating smell in the air which she later learnt was from opium smoke. The streets were mud, mud, and more mud. There's a well known saying about Guizhou Province:

The sky's not clear for three days on end,
The ground's not flat for three feet together.
No one has even three coppers for food.

Now it is a modern industrial city.

There were huge rats in the house where they lived; one night a rat bit Hongying's toes! The house had wooden floors and since it rained so much they collected buckets of rain water and washed the floors. They had to do all the work themselves. Hongying smoked a lot in those days!

Hongying was worried about Wuda: had it closed down or where had it moved to? Communications were hopelessly disrupted. So since she never liked to be idle, she asked if she might teach at the provincial high school; they asked her to take on 80 or 90 little boys, at the No.1 middle school - quite a challenge. In this disorderly situation, they had no text books; she taught them mainly by the direct method, demonstrating commands with actions: "Shut the door", "Pick up the book" and so on. The classroom had big windows and people going by the school would stare through them in amazement. They had never seen teaching like this before, so different from the usual learning by heart and reciting without understanding. She also tried the 'open-door' teaching which the Communists had started to use in the 'red

86

areas'. They learnt all sorts of practical skills such as gardening, carpentry, raising animals, and learnt the appropriate technical terms at the same time. Most of the children loved it: they clapped with enthusiasm - they saw book - learning transformed into something of practical use.

Mr Li was suspicious of Hongying because she was in her thirties and not married, but he accepted her eventually because he liked her method of teaching. This Mr Li had two sons and a daughter: the eldest son was with the Communists at their base in Yan'an; the younger one had just left school and longed to get away from home and study but this was impossible: in the Chinese tradition, at least one son had to stay with his parents and be responsible for them. The unmarried daughter was a good helpful person. Hongying used to give them English coaching in the evenings; at night she read in bed by candlelight.

Although what she was doing was useful, Hongying was anxious to get back to university teaching. By the end of March that year (1938), she was officially invited to re-join Wuda which had set itself up at Kiating in Sichuan. But the former Head of her department resigned almost immediately and his successor was a man who had made her life miserable in the past, so she too offered her resignation. It was not accepted however; instead, they sent her travelling expenses to come to Kiating (now Leshan).

She wrote to me unhappily before setting out in April: "Life in this place is dead, and I have been dead for such a long time. Shall be glad to go back to work....I feel exactly like a dog, who struggles to say something to his beloved master, and he never succeeds. My master is the poor humanity". (29 April 1938)

She started out by coach, and arrived in Chongqing after three days' journey through magnificent scenery. There she waited a while for the water to rise on the Yangzi River; steamers were cheaper and quicker than the coaches which travelled roundabout. Then she spent a week in Chengdu, at the West China Union University, and finally arrived in Kiating on June 16, still miserably depressed. "Sometimes the heart is so sad that the brain becomes dull and the mouth dumb", she wrote to me. She had a hard struggle to find somewhere to live, a single woman without special friends. Edith had gone back to Austria.

This was really the nadir for Hongying. For the first time in her life, she was losing hope. She felt that China was almost lost; the Wuhan area would fall any day (actually it didn't until October). "It is just unbearable agony to see on the one hand the sufferers, not for any wrong of their own, and on the other hand the learned, stupid and wicked......I literally have not the least energy or ambition to do anything....My heart has been sick for the last month or so."

Classes went on until the end of July, then from August till October, there was military training for all students. Hongying finally resigned and tried to find another job. She wrote to William Sewell, the Quaker Head of the Department of Chemistry at the West China Union University at Chengdu, who later became a good friend of hers, to tell him she was available for teaching. Sewell replied, asking her to come quickly to Chengdu as he was just going on overdue home leave to England, and was waiting for a replacement. Hongying was wonderfully happy with the offer. She arranged for Mingzhang to go to a Quaker school in Chongqing as a boarder (it was not expensive and said to be good) and moved her few belongings to Chengdu.

She wrote to me at the beginning of August, in a mood of euphoria. She had never felt free at Wuda, never fitted in or felt at ease. She speaks of having felt imprisoned, and of her present freedom of spirit. "I feel I have been a widow for the last two years and now remarried!" To celebrate her new state, she bought a piece of light green cotton material, patterned in what she saw as the Russian style, to make a summer dress - and sent me a sample of it. I still have this piece of cloth among my papers.

At West China Union University, Chengdu

So she joined the staff of the University in Chengdu, but it didn't fulfil her hopes. "At the bottom of every question, there is this, I am losing interest in life in general. China is in such a state and the world shows no sign of ever making an effort to save civilisation (democracy and freedom of thought - most precious to my mind). This institution is full of old heads and I can't push ahead. The students are like clay and wooden images. They do their text books and nothing else. I have been trying to move things a little bit and in consequence I offend everyone. You know I have no tact. So the sum total is despair."

The Head of Department, John Kao, perhaps being jealous of a supposedly better qualified person from 'down-river', or of her Oxford background, treated her badly. He taunted her with being an 'Overseas Chinese', which made her exceedingly angry. And she wasn't the only one he insulted: he used regularly to beat his Korean wife Kimmie, a nice person who had graduated from Yanjing. Hongying still remembers how, many years later, when she was married and living in Cambridge, Kimmie visited them with her young son, on her way back to China, and made delicious pickled cabbage for them! Luckily Kao soon obtained a grant to study in Canada and left. After this, the whole department

Hongying with Kimmie Kao in Hong Kong, 1976

got on well together. Hongying became Acting Head though she was never actually appointed, but she did all the administrative work, drawing up timetables, interviewing students and so on. She lived in the so-called Women's College which was really a dormitory for staff and students. She was also made a Director of extra-mural activities for women. A member of the Kuomintang Secret Service was Dean of Discipline for the whole University.

Using the Extra-mural Committee as cover, a Canadian called Earl Willmott, who had Communist sympathies, helped her organise twenty-five study groups under various religious guises, such as Bible Study and Hymn-singing. Some of these groups were formed only of students from the Women's College, and some were groups from the whole University. The group with which Hongying and Willmott were specially connected was called 'Science and Religion', but secretly they also discussed Marxism. Writing in later life to Earl's son Dick, she talked about his new method of discussion groups. "In the past, the person Jesus, long-bearded 'Son of God', 'Saviour of Mankind', meant nothing to me. Just a foreign story. But your father's method of collective thinking, questioning, probing, made the man Jesus alive and his teaching fresh and relevant to our personal and social life." (16 October 1985) At this time, she met David Crook, a British Communist, a teacher at St John's University in Shanghai. Because of the Japanese occupation, he had escaped to Chengdu as a refugee and he joined Hongying's group. It was he who gave them their Marxist grounding. When she read Communist literature, she used to draw the curtains in her room. A friend of hers who went to Chengdu in 1979 and visited the Museum of this University, saw there a note to the effect that 'Liao Hongying is a dangerous person and has to be watched'!

In those years she belonged to over 20 committees and was either Chairman or Secretary of many: Building Committee, Dormitory Committee, Food Committee, Physical Education Committee... She complained a great deal about all this administrative work.

There were new buildings for single women teachers. Hongying had a small office and a bedroom, though she slept winter and summer on the verandah; she thought it was more healthy, and besides, she was young then and didn't feel the cold so much. Among the other women teachers, there was always a lot of discussion about food - grumbles and complaints - but she simply didn't want to be bothered. The laundry was done for them - she had nothing to do but her own work. This was always her ideal - to have nothing in the world to think about except her studies.

The University Staff was a complete mixture. Next door to Hongying's room was the gym teacher. She plucked her eyebrows in a long straight line. She took about two hours every morning to dress; Hongying couldn't understand why she took so long to get up! Another of her neighbours was a teacher called Daisy Peng, who had collected millions of butterflies. She was infatuated with Dr Jiao, Head of Biology, but unfortunately he was already married.

At the end of her fourth year at Chengdu, Harry Silcock arrived from London to organise a post-war East Asian Conference, on behalf of the Quakers. He engaged Hongying to be the Organizing Secretary for the Conference in Chongqing; the Sichuan Quakers Yearly Meeting was to be responsible for her salary. She was fed up with the injustices at the University: the Dean of Discipline acted against the students instead of fighting for their rights. Thousands disappeared, including one of Hongying's students. The President was morally bankrupt. She still had to support her nephew at school and her University salary, devalued by the rampant inflation, was not enough for them both to live on. She resigned and went to Chongqing.

Chongqing and the expedition to Lanzhou

She started the correspondence in connection with the Conference; she had to pay for the stationery herself. There was constant squabbling between two leading Chinese Quakers. Nobody paid her salary or expenses. She wrote to Friends' House in London: 'No Quakerism in this Yearly Meeting' she complained. They replied that Sichuan ought not to host an international Conference. Besides there was no sign of the war's ending - it wouldn't be possible anyway. Hongying resigned from the thankless job.

At Chongqing, she lived in the YWCA. It was so damp that there were lime deposits on the walls, consequently she never felt well - was always having colds. The Zhengs, whom she had lived with in Guiyang, had also come to Chongqing now; the simple, sweet-natured wife insisted on Hongying's eating with them. From the shop opposite their home they fetched *doujiang* (bean milk) and *mantou* (steamed bread) for breakfast. The family cooked on the street, on a little cooker, and though there were never many dishes, they were all lovely. While living there, she got wind of what Mr Zheng was up to: he had got hold of a country girl and was using her as a concubine. Hongying persuaded the girl to stay with her in the YWCA and go to classes: she would protect her and see to her education - always Hongying's first concern. She begged the YWCA officials to help her save the girl, but one day, two soldiers came and carried her off, back to the Zhengs. The same thing had happened when she was living in Chengdu: she had tried to save another girl in this predicament and to educate her, but she had run away.

In Chongqing she found congenial work at last. The Sino-British Cooperation office had been set up by the Cambridge scientist, Joseph Needham (whom years before she had met in England) in the Embassy compound, and he asked her to help him. She worked there for a year (1942-43). But meanwhile she was becoming ill and weak from poor food and poor living conditions and was growing steadily weaker. There wasn't much to eat for anybody in China then, under the wartime conditions, but those without families fared even worse. Needham, who went all over

China to visit Universities and scientific institutions, was about to go by truck to Lanzhou, and since it was a government vehicle, there would be no travelling expenses - they would only have to pay for food. Joseph persuaded her that she was not fit to stay on in Chongqing - it would be far better for her health to go with him on account of the climate in the North-west. So she joined the expedition in the summer of 1943. The decision was to change her life.

From Lanzhou, Joseph with some of his staff, including his Chinese secretary, Huang Xingzong, and Rewi Alley, the New Zealander (who with the Englishman, George Hogg, had set up an Industrial Cooperative Training School at Shuangshipu) made a trip to the famous Buddhist caves at Dunhuang. Hongying couldn't go with them for lack of money; she stayed on in Lanzhou to teach in another Cooperative school. Also working with the Cooperatives in Lanzhou were Zhang Guanlian and his wife, a kind and hospitable couple, with whom she spent a lot of time. They once crossed the Yellow River on a sheepskin raft; later when it was frozen over, they could walk across. They really had great fun - a happy interlude at a stressful time.

Meeting Derek Bryan; their marriage

At the beginning of December, Needham and Rewi Alley returned from Dunhuang (where the breakdown of Needham's truck had enabled them to make an extended visit to the caves) to Lanzhou. Finding that the British Consul from Chengdu, whom he had met on the way up from Chongqing, was visiting Lanzhou, Needham suggested to Hongying that they should jointly pay him a courtesy call. He was staying, along with a few other foreign residents of Lanzhou,

94

including the US Consul and the British Congregationalist missionary J B Tayler, in the China Inland Mission.

"Call on an imperialist official - not likely!" Hongying exploded. Needham tried to persuade her: "We needn't really try to see him - just leave a card", but Hongying was adamant.

One day there was a meeting at the school, where Needham was to make a speech. The young British Consul was sitting in front; Hongying thought he was one of the missionaries. However, the Zhangs later organised a dinner for them all in a restaurant, and there she met Derek Bryan for the first time. So he was not a missionary after all! (She later remembered having had a letter from him two years earlier, addressed to 'Mr' Liao Hongying as Secretary of the Sino-British Cultural Association branch in Chengdu, about the then forthcoming visit of the British Ambassador. On arrival in Chengdu, the Ambassador gave a talk, interpreted into Chinese by Derek as his Private Secretary, at a big meeting there, one or two days before the Japanese attack at Pearl Harbour, on December 8, 1941, which abruptly cut short the visit.)

Because of the delay in Dunhuang, Needham decided to fly back to Chongqing, leaving the rest of the party to return by truck. Derek, who had come up by plane, decided to go back with them by road. One night on the journey, Hongying had a terrible cough which kept both of them awake. Next morning he produced a bowl of *beimu*, a traditional cough remedy, which was very comforting. "So he knows about Chinese medicine, more than I do", thought Hongying to herself. It was a long journey but she gradually got better; Derek looked after her all the time, putting his coat over her to keep her warm. The truck kept breaking down; pieces of it were actually tied together with string. On one occasion, when the truck was being repaired, they all went into a peasant's hut, where the occupants were burning the maize cobs to warm themselves. In the course of their conversation Derek remarked, "I was told that when the Communist troops passed this way, they did no harm to the people but actually helped them." This startled Hongying. "So he's not an imperialist official after all!" she thought, "he's on the side of the people!"

After that, they talked freely in the truck. She had been slightly reserved before and this discovery was a wonderful release. During one of their conversations it turned out that Derek had been one of Julian Bell's companions on their 1936 trip to the Tibetan borders. When they reached Chengdu, she gave Derek some dried Hami melon - a great delicacy.

A little later, Derek asked her to marry him. She refused at first, saying she was too old for him (by five years). However, she took him to meet her friends the Yangs, who were teaching outside Chongqing. Yang Xianyi (a young Chinese scholar) had become engaged to Gladys (daughter of J. B. Tayler and his wife) while they were fellow-students at Oxford. They had come back to marry in China, where they made a long and valued career as translators of Chinese literature into English. They were among Hongying's and Derek's closest friends in China. Gladys relates some impressions of the developing relationship in the spring of 1944.

"Xianyi and I were staying in Beipei on the Jialing River. Hongying brought Derek there to see us. They looked solemn; it started to rain. Hongying announced that she intended to live and die in China, but, she said, [Derek] mustn't ruin his career because of her. (In those days, diplomats were discouraged from marrying Chinese wives) so the atmosphere was hardly joyful."

One day at dinner with the Needhams, however, Hongying was persuaded. The difference in age didn't really matter, they urged her (Joseph Needham's wife Dorothy, also an FRS, was 4 years his senior) and Derek was such a good person and really cared about the Chinese people. The question of abode in connection with Hongying's nationality had evidently ceased to worry them. On 16 June 1944 they were married, after the Quaker fashion, at the West China Union University in Chengdu. Derek's leave was already overdue and in August they went to England together.

At a friend's wedding in Nanjing in 1949.

Part 5. Married life in England. Politics and teaching 1944 -

In mid-August 1944, they took a plane from Chongqing, flew over the 'Hump' and landed in Calcutta. The war was still on and all the planes had minimal furnishings; in their R.A.F. flying-boat they had to sit on the floor. At Gibraltar, another stop for refuelling, they bought bananas to bring home - an unbelievable luxury in wartime England. (I remember buying some of this wonderful fruit for my children after the war had ended, and being shocked at their lack of interest!) They landed at Poole and took the train to Waterloo and thence, via Liverpool Street to Norwich, Derek's home town.

Meeting the family

Derek's father came to meet them at the station on his bicycle - petrol was severely rationed, so no car. At Liverpool Street, Derek's attempt to buy chocolate had been met with an abrupt "Where's your coupons?" which he hadn't got. So another surprise!

His father was a highly respected dentist and his mother a very sociable person with many interests. It can't have been easy for them to accept Hongying, a Chinese, as a wife for their only son (Derek had three sisters) - she told me how self-conscious she felt. And she had more or less only the clothes she stood up in.

The Bryans had some help in the house for cleaning, but Hongying attempted to do the washing-up. There were so many pieces of china and cutlery! For breakfast, they had porridge and a cooked dish, coffee and toast and all the rest: it seemed like hundreds of pieces she had to wash up. And she broke things which couldn't be replaced in wartime - it was agony for her. Her upbringing in a Chinese family had been so different. In a Chinese big family, everything was done together. In Norwich, because she couldn't do the cooking and other domestic chores, she wanted to turn down the beds for the family, but this was not welcomed, which was really a cultural shock for her.

Derek's family lived on the outskirts of Norwich; in those days they would go by tram into the city. One day when Derek and Hongying accompanied his mother shopping, he paid the small fare for all three - it was quite cheap - but his mother wanted to pay back her share. This was another shock to Hongying. In China they would never have thought of doing such a thing, but she didn't like to make any comment. In later years, the relationship gradually became easier, and long before Derek's mother died, she used to say, "I couldn't have had a better daughter-in-law."

That autumn (1944), Derek and Hongying took a holiday with his parents in the Lake District. She speaks in a letter of the beauty and comfort there, "2 miles from our Little Braithwaite" of College days. But shortly before this, on the way up to Keswick, Hongying and Derek came to stay with me in Darlington, where my husband (a Czech refugee) was Scientific Officer to the Ordnance Factories in that region - a wartime appointment. This was our first meeting after more than seven years of momentous events. Though it was certainly joyful, it also felt strange in some indefinable way: we each had a husband now and I was absorbed in rearing two small children in wartime conditions, a grave little girl and a roly-poly boy.

Like a true Chinese, Hongying spoke little about her

marriage, nor was she in the least introspective, but she did confide in me in an October letter that year, in a tone of scientific enquiry, about how she had felt a change in her personality. "I seem to have lost a good deal of what I possessed before marriage, such as the spirit of independence and industriousness. Now I feel quite lazy and irresponsible and leave all responsibilities to Derek. I won't even carry any money or stamps with me... I wonder if this is general with women or quite peculiar to me, and is this temporary or permanent? Did you ever feel so, soon after you were married? Then the arrival of the first child brought you back your original qualities? I would like to know." (26 Oct. 1944)

Back in Norwich, Derek's leave was cut short (as it was wartime) and he was summoned to work in the Foreign Office in London. They stayed with Margery Fry in Clarendon Road. This was a great joy for Hongying - someone who knew and understood her. Hongying washed and darned Derek's socks; there were no nylon socks in those days. It was wartime and clothes were rationed - so many 'points' per person, she couldn't buy much. Poor Hongying used to cry over the washing. She knew married women had a hard life but thought it would be better in England which was so much more affluent, but it wasn't. There was a wartime mobilisation of all women from 19 to 45 years, and she was soon given work with the British Council. She became Head of the China Section, arranging the exchange of scholars between the two countries. It was mostly Chinese scholars coming to England then.

In May 1945 they were among the London crowds celebrating the end of the war (VE Day), but they had to wait till August (VJ Day) for victory over Japan. In July 1946 Hongying and Derek returned to China, to Nanjing, which had become the Capital again: Derek was Chinese Secretary at the Embassy.

Back at the Embassy in Nanjing

From 1941 to 1946, all Derek's belongings had been stored in Macao, in huge trunks. The linen was stained yellow, and so were the beautiful white shirts. There were huge piles of socks and good quality bath towels; they gave these to the servants. Many missionaries had lost all their possessions in the War, so they gave them the linen despite the bad colour. One trunk was half-full of old letters, menus and so on - they hardly kept anything - they seemed irrelevant. The clothing was in bad condition - all no use. The gramophone records had warped and were unusable. Hongying's own little gramophone and the records she had treasured, she had sold years ago, during the War, to buy necessities. They had to make a fresh start.

Hongying would have dearly liked to visit her home; she longed for it. But there was still banditry and no peace between the forces of Chiang Kaishek and Mao Zedong. Travelling was very difficult, especially for women. She was still working for the British Council, now under Dr. Silow at the Science Office. Professor Roxby, a well known geographer, was head of the organisation in China. From time to time she went to Shanghai meetings of the International Committee of the Chinese Industrial Co-operatives. She also went with Derek by RAF plane, accompanying the British Ambassador and some of his colleagues to Shandan and Chengdu, but there wasn't much travelling just then.

Hongying's social life in the diplomatic world was very hard for her with her simple background. There were many cocktail parties each week. "Sometimes I wish I were dead instead of going to them!" she wrote to me (in July 1948) with genuine passion. It was also terribly hot: Nanjing is one of the so-called 'three ovens' of China. The foreign diplomats in Nanjing included some distinguished figures. There was K.P.S.Menon, the first Indian High Commissioner after Independence, a product of the Indian Civil Service. He was succeeded as Ambassador by K.M.Panikkar, a brilliant person who had been advisor to one of the Indian Princely States and was both historian and poet. He wrote a pioneer work, '*Asia and Western Dominance*', and other historical books. Another gifted member of the circle at Nanjing was a figure known as 'old Trone', a Russian originally from Riga. He was an old Communist who could read Marx and Goethe in German, Lenin and Trotsky in Russian. (Much later, 1963, it was in his London house that a group, including Derek and Hongying, met to launch a serious Marxist-oriented publication, *Broadsheet*). These as well as a number of progressive Chinese opposed to the government, were some of the people whom Hongying and Derek were friendly with in Nanjing.

But they spread their net wide. Gladys Yang reminisces how they "had many friends, both Chinese and foreign. They were generous and outspoken, liked discussing the coming fall of the Kuomintang. Liao Hongying was a leading spirit in this, tireless and unfailingly tactful in roping in newcomers. She was skilled in summing up the political situation and presenting it forcefully to ordinary people". And, adds Gladys, "She deserves a lasting memorial... I am very proud to have known her".

China had by now relapsed into Civil War: Chiang Kaishek's Nationalist armies against the Communist forces led by Mao Zedong. (Chiang's Headquarters were in Nanjing). The contrast was painful for Hongying. She watched the students demonstrating and demanding a good education; the whole of society was gradually collapsing.

Young people disappeared at night. The ancient Chinese poet Du Fu had written:

> In the houses of the noblemen meat grows rank;
> At the roadside, the bones of the poor who have starved to death.

This was constantly being quoted. As they went about in the Embassy jeep, beggars would come to the windows and beg for money.

Nevertheless, December 1948 she describes as "the *happiest* Christmas of my life. The reason is, I have never seen peace in China since I was born. Now peace is not far off and the common man and woman will have a better livelihood for thousands of years" (30-12-48 Letter to I.H) As usual, her enthusiasm leapt ahead of the facts.In Nanjing she renewed an old friendship with Zeng Zhaoyue - a grand-daughter of the famous general Zeng Guofan (Tseng Kuo-fan). Zhaoyue had been studying archaeology and art history in London while Hongying was doing her research; she was now deputy-director of Nanjing National Museum, a very wonderful collection. Hongying told me how once when she had gone to see Zhaoyue, her friend had opened a drawer and found it stuffed with paper money - her salary. "Why don't you buy something with it?" asked Hongying. "In a short time it will be valueless", replied Zhaoyue: "my time is more valuable than this paper - I have no time for shopping!" Nominally Han Liwu was Head of the Museum, but Zhaoyue did all the organising. Actually she was quite frightened by the situation and around the time of Liberation came to stay with Hongying and Derek.

In their quarters at Nanjing, they had a cat and a dog. The dog, Tiddler, was a mongrel dachshund, inherited from a British business family who lived next door and were going on home leave. The cat came as a kitten from someone in

Ginling Women's College; it was a tortoiseshell and very intelligent. Dog and cat played and fought and slept in the same basket. Hongying called the cat 'Guerrilla' and the dog 'Kuomintang'. This story appeared in one of the Hong Kong Chinese newspapers after they had passed through on their way home in 1951; it may have been one of the counts against them. The dog used to steal the cat's food while the cat would eat anything, including peanuts. One day she ate 32 peanuts and was sick and never ate them again - she was really intelligent! When she was about to have kittens, she let Hongying stroke her when she was in pain but wouldn't let her touch the kittens at first. They took her in a basket to Beijing when the Embassy moved there in February 1950, but they had to give the dog away.

They spent a fruitful and exciting year in Nanjing under a Chargé d'Affaires. The group of negotiating representatives was relatively small but Hongying and Derek had quite a number of Chinese contacts. Although ordinary communications were cut off and they were not allowed to travel outside the city limits, there was plenty of new life springing up: new films, new plays, in that atmosphere of jubilation.

They had expected to be in Beijing by Christmas 1949, and they were to return to the huge Embassy compound. While waiting for word from London that Britain had recognised the new regime, and in a mood of elation, Hongying went shopping with Derek and bought warm material to make her winter clothes for use in the North.

In February 1950, the British diplomatic staff moved to Beijing. The British Council, for which Hongying had been working, was restricted in what it could do after Liberation so she took part in a Study Group of Chinese women, the wives of professional people. They concentrated on discussion of U.S. imperialism and the United Nations.

At the beginning of 1951, they left China on home leave; travelling was easier then, after the country had been liberated. On 3 May it snowed as they were on their way to Norfolk. They had no home of their own as yet so they took their luggage to Derek's parents in Norwich, where it was stored in the attic. There were a few antiques which they had collected, but they had bought little compared with some people. They spent a few months in Norwich, partly travelling round to visit Derek's relatives.

Derek's retirement from the Foreign Office. London and the Cambridge interlude

The original expectation had been that they would return to China sometime in September or October 1951, but before then, Derek was called to the Foreign Office to discuss his future. The usual rule, that a Foreign Service officer whose wife was not British, should not be posted to her native country, had not been followed in 1946, and they felt quite confident of being able to return. However, the Foreign Office felt that Derek had become too pro-Chinese and Hongying too anti-American. The end of the Labour government in Britain was also a period of maximum US pressure, and the defection of Donald Maclean was still fresh in people's minds; he had escaped to Moscow in May 1951.

So after a lot of discussion, it was proposed to send Derek to Peru as Commercial Secretary for two years. He asked if he was likely later to be posted to China again, or alternatively work in London, but the authorities held out no hope for this. Hongying said she was ready to go with him to Lima if necessary, but Derek was not willing for them to be separated from China in this way, and decided to opt for early retirement. This took effect in February 1952. Impossible to imagine what a difficult decision this must have been for them both, though pondering over might-have-beens was never a characteristic of either.

Chinese Book Exhibition, early 1950s.

They rented a flat in Mountview Road, North London, from a very orthodox Jewish couple. They had to do their own catering for the first time and some food was still rationed. They used to scour the shops for unrationed tinned food and come home with arms full of tins.

Hongying was urging Derek to take up some research. **Study** has always been of pre-eminent importance to her, ever since she started to recite after her father when she was two years old. In her home now, you would find old volumes of the Confucian classics, reverently cared for, in one of her bookcases; in another, the Works of Mao Zedong and modern analyses of Communist theory. She never forgot her roots in her concern for the present, and this was perhaps a main source of her strength.

Derek now began to attend classes at the School of Oriental and African Studies, in classical Chinese, including the first five Chapters of the *Red Chamber Dream*, expounded by John Chinnery (later founder of the Chinese School at Edinburgh University) and a few Chapters of the *Analects* of Confucius (*Lun Yu*) taught by A. C. Graham (later Professor at the School of Oriental and African Studies). These and some other classes which he followed for a couple of terms were intended to equip him for sinological research.

In the autumn of 1952, they decided to move to Cambridge, as a quieter place to study. They bought a small terrace house in Victoria Street - the first home of their own since they married - and furnished it simply. Derek had decided to return to his Alma Mater, to try to get a Ph.D. in Chinese Studies; he chose for his subject Lu Xun, the greatest modern Chinese writer. S. I. Hsiung, adapter of the play *Lady Precious Stream*, who lived in Oxford, came once a week to Cambridge and was supposed to be Derek's supervisor, but in fact he gave very little guidance. So after less than a year, Derek changed his subject to the mid-19th century revolt of the Taipings against the Manchu Dynasty. Again there was no guidance; Professor Haloun, a Czech sinologist, had died and his successor, Professor Pulleyblank, had not yet been appointed. Derek read the Jardine-Matheson archives in the Cambridge University Library, but found little about the Taipings.

But what, it may be asked, was Hongying doing all this time, from 1952 till April 1956, when they sold their home in Cambridge and returned to London? Domestic work, 'keeping house' as we know, positively repelled her. "I dread domestic drudgery more than anything in life!" she had written to me once. In December 1954, one of her letters explained with some distress: "I feel we are not doing the right thing in these years."

They had made another attempt to return to China, since both felt they could certainly be useful. They had enquired of Huan Xiang, (the Chinese Chargé d'Affaires newly appointed to Britain as a result of the limited détente achieved by Zhou Enlai and Eden at the Geneva Conference of 1954) whether they could go back and work for China in some capacity. But Huan told Derek that the Chinese authorities did not want to risk damaging their improved relations by employing a previous British official. He might be considered by either side to be a political spy. The case of Donald Maclean (who incidentally had been a schoolfellow of Derek's at Gresham's) was cited once more.

So they started to carry out speaking engagements together and separately to United Nations Association branches, schools, Townswomen's Guilds and Trades Union branches (though these latter she found the most unresponsive; they were not political but were only interested in wages, she said). Although they made conscientous and thorough preparations, she continued to be uneasy. She felt Derek ought to be devoting himself to serious academic study while he himself thought it his duty to combat the lies about China, fed to the British public at that time.

What really interested him was the newly-formed Britain-China Friendship Association. He became Secretary of the active Cambridge Branch and spent more time on this work than on his less than whole-hearted attempts at academic research which were getting nowhere. Hongying said he was like John the Baptist, "a voice crying in the Wilderness" unable to influence the process of the cold war, something he had hardly expected to achieve! She couldn't settle as long as he wasn't fruitfully occupied or contented. In addition, she was beginning to find the Cambridge climate didn't suit her; it was damp and cold with winds blowing in off the Fens. She was frequently ill.

So, prompted by friends, they moved back to London in the Spring of 1956, and bought a spacious Edwardian house, divided into two flats, in Holden Road, North Finchley. It had a large, beautiful but neglected garden (which they struggled with for years until Derek's sister moved in downstairs and started to transform it). The Dollis Brook, swirling and bubbling, girded it at the end. Here they unpacked their books, Chinese scrolls, their few pieces of antique furniture and rugs and augmented them with various serviceable pieces bought in the neighbourhood. Hongying spoke of the "mental agony of moving house" and that she would "never move again as long as she lived". But this was only her characteristic attitude to life in general, on which she always held decided views but frequently had to modify them later.

1956 onwards: life in London

Derek having abandoned his attempts at academic research, they both threw themselves with energy into the task of telling anyone interested about the "New China". Derek now worked part-time for a trade magazine (*Far East Trade*) and also taught some evening classes in Chinese at Princeton College of Language and Commerce (later amalgamated with a law school from South London to become the Holborn College of Law, Languages and Commerce). To these activities he added some courses and lectures on China for the Workers' Educational Association and the Cambridge Extra-Mural Board in North London.

But what absorbed most of their energies was trying to explain and defend the young People's Republic and its policies in a Britain that was largely hostile, or at least ignorant of the issues. They did this particularly through the Britain-China Friendship Association which had been started soon after the establishment of the People's Republic of China, and in the cold war climate of the time was supported almost entirely by the Left.

It may be wondered why Hongying didn't decide to teach the subject for which she had studied and researched - agricultural chemistry, or at least some allied subject. In fact, when they first settled in England, some of Hongying's friends had urged her, "why not come and teach Science?" Many British science teachers had been killed in the war; there would have been a real opening for her. But she felt that this was not of first importance; it was not the job for which she was uniquely suited and which she felt it her duty to do - to talk about her country. The British tamely followed the US, the Third World countries were all anti-China because controlled by CIA bribery, the US controlled the

Speaking at a meeting of the Business and Professional Women's Guild, c. 1960

United Nations' voting box. So she decided to give the greater part of her time to explaining the Chinese Revolution.

New Year 1957 found her depressed. She complains of feeling 'miserably tired with housework' of having 'aged rapidly' (her first mention of ageing in her letters) and - of not having borne children. This was a very Chinese feeling and one which she rarely alluded to. They were private complaints which came from her heart: to the outside world she was increasingly in demand as a speaker.

She travelled all over London and up and down the country to talk and lecture. Beth Bailey (Allan) remembers her coming to the Finchley Quaker Meeting when she herself was quite small. Hongying told the children about life in

China, and taught them how to eat with chopsticks out of porcelain bowls. She made sure that they received copies of *China Reconstructs*, an illustrated magazine about the building of the new People's Republic, so that Beth was aware since childhood of China as a brave and lively country. Another friend, Joan Browne, tells how fascinated the audience (a large crowd at the Coventry Teachers' Training College) were by tales of Hongying's family; her father, the traditional Chinese teacher, and her grandmother who used to take her round the village on her back when she was little; but especially when she began to write Chinese characters on the blackboard and explain how they had been simplified. Hongying continued to speak, at the various organisations, all through the 50s and 60s, but by the end of the 60s the whole world situation had changed. Many Third World countries had come to see through US policy; British policy changed too: many colonies were freed; the People's Republic of China was firmly established. In 1971 China was at last voted into its rightful place at the United Nations. China began to open up to British visitors and the demand fell off for that kind of speaking, because so much information was already available. At this point, Hongying gave it up.

The Britain-China Friendship Association and Friends of China

Here it may be appropriate to say something more about the Britain-China Friendship Association (which they both had previously joined in 1951 when they returned to London from China) and on which Derek had spent so much time when they lived in Cambridge.

The BCFA had been set up late in 1949; it was the

only British friendship organisation in the China field and formed a focus for all those who wanted to show active support for the newly liberated Chinese. The leading role was played by the British Communists. At that time, the press and public opinion were almost uniformly hostile: the BCFA attempted to spread the facts about the Korean War (in which British troops, under the banner of the United Nations, were fighting the Chinese in Korea), about Taiwan, China's position in the United Nations, the rights of China in the border clashes with India in 1959 and the brief war of 1962, in which the British sided with India.

All through most of the fifties, under the Sino-Soviet Treaty of Friendship and Co-operation, economic aid in the form of loans, industrial materials and technical expertise, were offered to China by the Soviet Union. Soviet technicians and designers came in their thousands to help build the new Communist State. But already in 1956, a beginning of the Sino-Soviet split, due largely to ideological differences, had become apparent. The Great Leap Forward and the People's Communes starting in 1958, initially so full of hope for the Chinese, had been laughed to scorn by Khruschev, and the British were inclined to agree. Hongying was active in the BCFA all this time.

In 1960, Khruschev suddenly withdrew all the technicians and engineers who were working in China on major industrial projects, and also refused to share with the Chinese any atomic weapons secrets. It turned out that there were irreconcilable contradictions between the Communist parties of the Soviet Union and China, and the BCFA declined to enter the controversy between the supporters of either party. There seemed to be a policy of silence in any issue involving dispute between the two, but in fact the quarrel had been festering within the organisation for several years.

One Saturday in early May 1964, the BCFA held a fateful AGM. It was a difficult meeting to run, and the Chairman didn't make a very good job of it, appearing to favour the pro-Soviet faction who had clearly stacked it. These members cared little for China's interests and, after furious debates, won the day. Hongying and Derek were not the only ones to feel bitterly disappointed, frustrated and angry. Some of their friends, meeting afterwards in a tea shop, overheard Palme Dutt, a Soviet supporter, say to his companions, "Well, we managed that meeting well and carried all our resolutions!".

This was virtually the end of BCFA though not the end of support for China in Britain.

The effect of the Sino-Soviet split, not only on the British Communists but on other Left-wing organisations had been shattering, as, on a different but related level, had been the Khruschev revelations about Stalin (1954), the invasion of Hungary (1956) and as were to be, some years later, the invasion of Czechoslovakia (1968). The turmoil and political ferment which were caused within the Communist Parties were immense.

Effects were largely negative, but although there was a desperate hope that out of the Khruschev revelations a more humane kind of Communism might emerge in the Soviet Union, with the accession of Brezhnev it was realised that a radical overhaul of the Communist Party from within was about to be crushed, and it was indeed lost forever. In this extremely depressing situation, China seemed, in Hongying's words, "like the growing light in this dark world".

Thousands of British Communists had left the Party round about this time, some 'because of Hungary' but others for a variety of other reasons, so that there was a large number of committed Communists floating about, looking for a focus, a 'home'. Into this sense of desolation broke the inspiring leadership of Mao Zedong and Zhou Enlai. It seemed, there was space for a new organisation in Britain to spread the Chinese viewpoint; to show how a fresh kind of socialism could be built, even in a backward country like China, and that Mao's ideas, though primarily addressed to China's situation, contained the basic truths of Marxism and could well take sympathetic root in Britain.

So through the early summer and the autumn of 1964, a small group of people, including Hongying and Derek, met and discussed, sometimes into the night, the possibility of setting up this new body. Out of their discussions grew the Friends of China, small local groups of 20 or 30 people at first, one in Cambridge, in Cheltenham, Manchester, the East End and various other places in London, such as Merton. Hongying always took the trouble to help these local organisations that were trying to get established. At the inaugural meeting of the Merton branch in June or July 1964, where Alex Tudor-Hart and John Lloyd were the leading spirits, she was the main speaker. Her subject, as far as John can remember, was the history of the Chinese Communist Party and she spoke well. She seemed always able to hold an audience with her obvious sincerity and directness. She also made a very favourable impression on many people who were not particularly 'political'. And she appealed especially to the young, who at that time were caught up in a wave of idealism. Some sober souls thought that she looked at China through glasses that were too rosy, especially when the Cultural Revolution got out of hand. But we were all rather like that then: China seemed uniquely able to offer hope in a confused world.

A return visit to China 1959.
New life in the People's Republic

But this is anticipating events. While the polemic between China and the Soviet Union was heating up, in September 1959 a British cultural group was invited to China through the BCFA for the tenth anniversary celebrations of the founding of the People's Republic. It was composed of Herbert Read, the author and art critic; the scientist Dorothy Hodgkin; and Professor Garner from Rothamsted Experimental Station, accompanied by Derek and Hongying. They flew to Moscow and from there to Beijing on a Soviet jet. It was on this visit that they travelled down the Yangzi by boat through the famous Three Gorges, from Chongqing to Wuhan - familiar scenes from Hongying's past. The boat was pretty dirty, but the scenery was absolutely breath-taking.

This was Hongying's first return to her homeland since her marriage; also her first living contact with China since Liberation - an intense emotional experience. In those ten years, tremendous progress had been made, more notably in the cities with China's burgeoning industry still supported by the co-operation of the Soviet Union. This was the time of the Great Leap Forward and also the Three Hard Years, 1959-61, when flood, drought and famine tested the will and steadfastness of the people. Hongying noted of this time that they found villagers still burning vegetable oil with primitive wicks of rushes to light their homes, some village children were still going barefoot in summer, just as she had known in her childhood, and they were still milling grain laboriously by hand. Eighteen months later, most was done by electricity, wind or water power. At the same time, in many a town and village, she experienced a feeling of ease - really liberation and self-confidence in the ordinary people which she hadn't known before.

116

This was perhaps especially noticeable in the women. They were freeing themselves from the perpetual drudgery of housework and cooking and also from the unrelieved duties of child-minding (nurseries and crèches attached to the factories in the cities and to the Communes in the countryside). They were beginning to get education and were able to discuss the management of their affairs. "China is now having another revolution", she had written in September 1958, "which will be another very important landmark in the history of mankind. The Agricultural Co-operatives are merging into People's Communes in which women - peasant women, do not have to do their own cooking, laundry etc. Restaurants, public service (units) are being established, plenty of them, in every village all over China." (22.9.58) Unfortunately this was an example of the wishful thinking of the period, but where her heart was engaged, Hongying was always single-minded and could overlook objections.

Hongying's second elder sister-in-law, when her daughter-in-law was expecting her first baby, had travelled alone from the family home in Changting, by bus, train and steamer to Chengdu - a thousand miles! In her youth, nobody would have believed this possible for a woman alone. Then, she had never travelled without someone to look after her.

Mingzhang, the boy whose education Hongying had supervised for 17 years, was now a lecturer in Anatomy in Sichuan Medical College. This had grown from a few hundred students in 1952 to 4,000 in 1958. In a letter to Gertrude Roland (13.1.85) she explains how she had guided him towards medicine to compensate for having rejected that discipline herself. "Er-Ge wanted me to be a *doctor*. [But] no, I wanted to be a teacher like father and two [of my] brothers. So I put his son into a medical college - to answer his wish for me". This year, 1959, he was taking part in the *xia fang* - the 'going to the country'. He and some of his fellow staff members and a number of students went to some of the surrounding villages to live and work among the peasants for several months at a time. In the morning, they held their own classes and during the day worked with the peasants on the farms. In the evenings they held classes for the country people in simple science, public health, discussions on political questions, singing and dancing and other topics. The ordinary people acquired an introductory knowledge of general education; the academics found the practical experience made their studies come alive and they also gained an alertness and freshness of insight which helped them later in their research. Many have testified to this, though others complained they were wasting precious years.

Another of her nephews (her sister's son), a brilliant historian in Changchun, NE China, could only be spared from his administrative duties at his University for short periods during vacations, to go down to the villages. In 1959, together with some colleagues and students, he had gone to his University farm to dig a big pond for fish breeding, so that they could become self-sufficient in fish. Hongying was confident that they would have gone on to build a large piggery and poultry farm as well.

At Chongqing they visited an excellent commune, specializing in fish, cows and poultry. A vice-chairwoman showed them round: what a contrast with the sheltered life, Hongying's mother had passed within the family courtyard! Women were beginning to take a fuller place in society.

The delegation returned to England at the end of the month, but Derek and Hongying stayed behind. Hongying wanted to visit her hometown of Changting, though Derek wasn't allowed to accompany her. Only certain cities were open to foreigners at that time and Fujian was really a no-go area, being so close to Taiwan. Derek stayed on in Beijing with their close friends, Gladys Yang and her husband Yang Hsianyi, both of whom worked for the Foreign Languages Press. Hongying herself had to fight for the permission to go home; they waited a long time in Beijing for this. The Cultural Association tried to help - they said they would pay a Party member to go with her. "You don't trust me!" she protested. In the end they let her go alone. This was her first unfortunate encounter with bureaucracy - a side of Chinese Communism which persists to this day.

She spent only five days in Changting. Her eldest sister-in-law took her around to visit friends in the villages. They went out one day without locking the door; Hongying was amazed - in the old days, they wouldn't have left a broken bottle outside for fear of robbers. "Don't you know - we've been liberated!" said her sister-in-law. Hongying realised that this trust was a sign of Communist society. She met some villagers she had known slightly when she was a girl, such as the neighbour who had introduced her to Sunday School. They talked about the new life. There was plenty in her farmyard; in 1955 and 1956 there had been good post-Liberation welfare and things seemed to be going well. After meeting a young niece of 20, Hongying said she should have a silk-padded gown for her wedding, so they went to the tailor to order it. Her family had engaged her to someone she didn't know, but she herself had fallen in love with a young teacher. She could only break her engagement by paying $300; Hongying sent this to her later and she married the young man of her heart and was happy.

In her booklet, '*The World Belongs to All*', written (with Derek) after this first return to China, and published privately in 1960, Hongying captures the poignancy of her feelings in her discussions with Mingli, a young unmarried niece - daughter of her third brother and his wife, who was working enthusiastically on a People's Commune, training peasant women to be teachers in Nursery School, Kindergarten and Primary School. At 21, she had experienced life before Liberation but was then learning to 'Serve the People'. "I did not succeed in suppressing the mixture of feelings inside me", wrote Hongying, - "the joy for them and sadness for myself, that I was not able to participate in their creative work". No matter that she was working tirelessly in England for a true understanding of her homeland, not to have been able to take part in the building of socialism there must have been a bitter, unavailing regret. Stoically she never spoke of this to me in all the years I knew her. This is how she captures the scene as she leaves Fujian for Beijing: "It was early in the morning and the sun was not too warm yet. The hills on one side of the valley were in sunshine and the young trees on the formerly barren red earth seemed to have a peculiar power to draw me close to them. There were few people about the village streets but more people walking about the fields with various farm implements on their shoulders or under their arms. I tried hard to take in the picture, hoping to keep a few landmarks in my mind's eye, as something extremely precious, memories of this place which I had known so well in my youth."

Teaching at the Polytechnic of Central London

After she returned to Beijing and rejoined Derek, they travelled back to England by the Trans-Siberian Railway, spending five days in Leningrad as the guests of Russian friends. These were the sisters Serafimova, Masha and Lisa, "the most generous and warm-hearted people I have ever known", as Hongying describes them enthusiastically. She had come to hear of them through a Russian teacher (Vera) at the Foreign Languages Institute in Beijing, where David Crook, a colleague of Hongying's at Chengdu during the War, was also teaching. Vera spoke a lot about her two Russian friends in Leningrad.

Hongying was tremendously elated as a result of this visit. She was fascinated by the Soviet Union, and Russian, she thought, was a most beautiful language. She was convinced that language was the key to the understanding of a people. On her return to England, she began a correspondence with Masha and kept it up for many years. She sent her gifts of stockings, pants and petticoats - practical presents; Masha sent her back caviar. Hongying joined a Russian class of 10 or 12 people, run by a young Englishman, near where she lived in Finchley. She got as far as passing her 'O' level and wanted to go on, but couldn't find anywhere in the neighbourhood where she could learn to *speak*. Besides, other more pressing work intervened and she decided to give it up. In this period of the Thaw, the mid '50s, many people were keen to take up Russian out of general interest and sympathy, and no doubt there was an element of this for Hongying. And the visit by the Moscow Theatre in June 1958 had roused her intense enthusiasm too. It was "full of new ideas. I don't mean new ideas in the big but abstract and vague intellectual sense, but in the sense that we have fresh outlook and new light on ordinary things that we have to do from day to day."

Whether the British public was fascinated by China (the visit, in 1955, of the brilliant Peking Opera, for instance, amazed London theatre-goers), or felt fear of the burgeoning socialist republic on the other side of the world, an intense interest in China - or curiosity - was inescapable. It is not surprising, therefore, that this should also find an outlet in the academic world. In the autumn of 1963, Derek began teaching Chinese at the Holborn College, (one day a week at first) in what was to become the Language School of the Polytechnic of Central London. A little later, Hongying joined him. In the middle 60s and the 70s, the demand for Chinese courses expanded steadily until in 1974 Modern Chinese was introduced into the Language Degree Course - a very different matter from the degrees in Classical Chinese at Oxbridge. Derek was by then in charge of the Chinese Section, and Hongying an energetic and inspiring teacher. She taught Chinese Literature with some verve, and also ran a course for interpreters (simultaneous translation) which was quite demanding. I was also in London then and decided to take up Modern Chinese. I shall always remember the slightly severe figure of this small Chinese woman, who refused to accept sloppy thinking but who yet managed to mix enjoyment with her strenuous instruction. I always emerged from her classes on a high note.

The China Policy Study Group - The Broadsheet

Alongside their teaching was their uninterrupted political writing and organising. As a counter to the official British Communist pro-Soviet Line, which had submerged the BCFA, a new group was to represent the Chinese viewpoint, the Chinese side of the polemic. They called themselves the China Policy Study Group and their publication which came out monthly, *The Broadsheet*.

The first meeting of the group was in July 1963;

publication of *The Broadsheet* started in 1964. They were a very serious, very political organisation, often arguing long over a single word - to get it exactly right. Hongying said, they showed extreme individualism in their criticism of one another's writing - "Nobody likes anyone else's articles," she wrote in one of her numerous notebooks (21.6.76) but also a little earlier that month, how someone had reported to her, "Felix Greene greatly values your clear, correct political stand"* (Felix later played a leading role in a parallel organisation, the Society for Anglo-Chinese Understanding). Hongying in fact wrote some of the Broadsheet editorials; a few were described as "outstanding". She had a wonderfully clear mind and expressed her ideas with logic, directness and in plain language that all could understand. As always, she was the educator.

Among those who originally formed the core group for the *Broadsheet* were Percy Timberlake, an economist and consultant on China trade; Tana Sayers who had worked at *Xinhua* the Chinese News Agency in London and later in China; the architect Colin Penn and his wife Virginia, (assistant secretary of the BCFA for many years) both of whom had worked for *Xinhua* in Peking; the writer William Ash and his wife Ranjana from Bengal, and Peter Townsend, author of *China Phoenix*. Their organisation was a democratic one; they had no officials (apart from a treasurer) and almost all their articles were unsigned. The group met at first in one another's homes, but later mainly at the Bryans in

---

* Regarding these notebooks, Hongying in her insatiable eagerness for knowledge, accumulated an incredible number of them. She always kept a small one in her handbag, in which she jotted down interesting items and she had also a series of exercise books with a record of her correspondence - a wide one - in and out, in English or Chinese, and a summary of the important points inscribed in her neat, even hand.

Holden Road. Ranjana remembers how they would all sit around a big table and decide who was to write what, and would vehemently criticise the results. "Hongying was a splendid hostess," said Ranjana, "she did us proud, with excellent 'eats' to help out our endless discussions. She had a great warmth of manner, was endlessly generous with time, money, food, whatever was needed. If you were upset, she would make time to listen and help." What Ranjana remembers about her particularly was her simplicity, in her home, in her daily doings. More than anyone she knew, Hongying lived out her principles. One of her College friends, Joan Browne, remembers how she went with Hongying and Derek to the great Chinese Exhibition at Burlington House, and they had all gone afterwards to Bertorelli's in Charlotte Street for a meal. Hongying looked at the Menu and remarked, quite crossly, "We oughtn't to have come here Joan, its too expensive for us!" So typical of Hongying who was the very opposite of mean - boundlessly generous, but who couldn't bear senseless extravagance. Plenty of simple, wholesome food was all she ever provided - or wanted.

Some of her new friends felt she must be really poor, to judge from her clothes, but when she attended social functions, at the Chinese Embassy for instance, she put on lovely Chinese dresses and jackets. It was just that she despised 'show' and fashion, and as long as her clothing was clean and decent, she didn't mind how she looked for everyday, for her working life.

About her home, I always remember the sparkling white sheets on the spare bed and the warm dry towels put out for my use. Then the comfortable desk or writing table under the bedroom window, fixed up with all the writing instruments (in a jam jar) and a good supply of rough paper clipped together, and horse-brass for a paper-weight. On the armchair in winter, a rug folded lengthways and pinned at intervals with large safety-pins, to make a bag for my legs. One was always expected to do some *study* when visiting. There were plenty of books too, and a serviceable reading-lamp, not like the rushes or the candles with which she had had to make do in China during her childhood.

On another tack, I can speak of a social characteristic which stems from her Chineseness: the belief that "nothing in the world is single", that a happy ending in marriage must be the desire of every young person (followed by the production of babies). At any rate, starting from her Oxford days, she became known in her circle as a matchmaker, and is proud of the various marriages which she brought about. We often teased her for this! Two of her satisfied customers gave her a huge block of cheese (a favourite food) to thank her for their happy union. John Lloyd remembers how she tried to fix him up with a young wife. "Lots of elderly men in China do this", she said: "it gives them new liveliness - invigorates them!".

The Society for Anglo-Chinese Understanding

Around the time when the China Policy Study Group (more often known as the Broadsheet group) was developing and the small groups of Friends of China were having a pronounced though limited impact, the demand grew for an organisation with a much broader appeal and a wider membership, one which would not be limited to political and economic interests, but would involve cultural and social activities as well. This ultimately emerged as the Society for Anglo-Chinese Understanding (SACU), with the emphasis on friendship through understanding. (The character for Friendship, calligraphied by a distinguished Chinese artist, Fang Zhaoling, for SACU, was adopted by many friendship organisations internationally).

But the birth was not easy. Furious debates broke out between the SACU supporters and the Friends of China. Real differences of principle were sharpened by personality clashes and differences in background and outlook. Although all were left-wing and many were Marxist in both camps, some were working-class and others, like Jack Perry and Roland Berger were successful businessmen and trade consultants, whereas people like Joan Robinson, the Cambridge economist, and Joseph Needham were distinguished academics.

Again they differed in organisational principles. Whereas the Friends of China favoured the mass line and a democratic style, the SACU promoters proposed a nationwide organisation with many important names as sponsors. The Friends of China included some who were sectarian and intolerant - they couldn't distinguish between support for Marxism-Leninism and friendship with the Chinese people, whereas the SACU followers wanted a forum where the Chinese viewpoint could be studied but where they would not be expected to take political action. And they were admittedly superior in intellectual and financial resources.

In the debate between these two, Hongying came down strongly on the side of SACU. Her influence was considerable because she was widely respected for her knowledge of Chinese culture as well as the political thought, and for her obvious sincerity. The Chinese authorities also viewed the project favourably.

In 1964 a contingent of China stalwarts were invited to China for the 15th anniversary celebrations of the founding of the People's Republic. (Derek and Hongying had also been invited but were not free to go.) There were discussions about the proposal with the Friendship Association: it received enthusiastic support. Later that year until the following May, preparations went on including full time secretarial work. A long list of distinguished sponsors was drawn up; Roland Berger did a big PR job for the organisation. Letters went out to people in all walks of life: politicians, trades union leaders, scientists, artists, writers, dons, economists, radio and TV personalities; it was obviously not to be a grass-roots organisation like the Broadsheet group and the Friends of China.

The inaugural meeting was held on 15 May 1965 at Church House Westminster, meeting place of the Church of England Synod. One couldn't get more 'Establishment' than that! The organisers were actually trying to break away from association with the Communist Party and present a broad aspect to the British public. Dr Joseph Needham, now recognised as the great historian of Chinese science, took the Chair. Derek was appointed General Secretary, a position which he filled for over two years; later he succeeded Needham as Chairman. Hongying, perhaps because she mistrusted her command of English, worked more in the background.

But the Society which had opened on such a high note soon ran into trouble, or rather China did, in the eyes of the British public. By 1966, the Cultural Revolution was in full swing and gathering momentum. By 1967 the Chinese Embassy staff were battling with police in London while the British Embassy in Beijing was burnt down. Support for China rapidly fell away and there was wholesale desertion of the Chinese cause by people in general.

Most of the SACU members were loyal to China.

127

They bought their Little Red Books, diminutive books in red plastic covers to withstand hard wear. They discussed and disputed. At the inaugural meeting of the Hampstead Branch, Hongying spoke on 'Going to the Country', one of the procedures recommended for curing intellectuals of their feelings of superiority.

Further visits to China

In 1971, some years after their last visit, Hongying and Derek were again invited to China by the Chinese authorities. They went in a small group with the writer Roger Howard. Hongying didn't want to go at first; she didn't like

Meeting the writer Guo Muoro in Beijing, 1971.

128

just to tag along simply as Derek's wife, but the Embassy people assured her, she was being invited on her own merits. They visited Dazhai (the model Commune), Yan'an (the Red base during the war against Japan), Tianjin, Nanjing,Shanghai and other places.

They were again invited to China through SACU, along with three others, in 1975 and were able to go to Changting - Derek was given permission this time, but they had to stay in the official Guest House. At her old home, there were four generations of the Liao family under one roof (as the writer Lao She had described in his novel of that name). At that time, her eldest brother and two of her three sisters-in-law were still living - about 50 people altogether. Hongying has an amazing photograph of them all. When she and Derek returned about ten years later (1986), the only member of Hongying's generation was her eldest sister-in-law (Da-Sao), an old woman of 88 who didn't recognise anybody any more. Her elder brother, who like so many intellectuals and others had been victimised in the early stages of the Cultural Revolution, had been rehabilitated. The money which Hongying and Derek had sent from time to time had been kept back by the authorities; then it was distributed to the family members.

In 1975 Beijing had informed the Party people at Changting of their intended arrival; a big dinner was given for them and there was another feast at home. But the time was much too short - only two days and nights squeezed out of a 3-week delegation visit. Hongying felt miserable; it was all too formal, not a proper homecoming. She wanted to provide some money for setting up local industries, in memory of her father and of her second brother, who had died in Singapore in 1939 during the war. She phoned Beijing but they were simply evasive - said it couldn't be done just then. Hongying was dreadfully disappointed.

She had begun to realise how good her eldest brother was, how in the Cultural Revolution, he had spoken up, defending people, and she began to respect him. Now, when they said good-bye, both were in tears. "We shall come back to celebrate your 90th birthday" she said, but before she could make good her promise, the following April (1976) he had died.

By the time of their next visit, the Chinese government's policy had changed. The ailing Mao Zedong had died in 1976 and been succeeded by Hua Guofeng. To her Russian friends, Lisa and Masha, she wrote that "China is very different now. People are full of energy and self-confidence and free to discuss national and international questions". "Everything seems shining and full of light" she wrote to me in May, 1979.

English began to be in demand. Hongying and Derek received an invitation to come to China for six months (May till October 1979) to teach English at Fuzhou and Xiamen. This was much more satisfactory for her. She was never content simply with sight-seeing, and being part of a delegation but wanted to do something *useful*. She complained that they were being treated as tourists. However the invitation evoked a confusion of feelings, as she wrote to her friend William Sewell: "This is the first time of going among the people again after three decades of world-shaking events separating us. The 30 years of deep-going political education have so penetrated their social and spiritual being that it is impossible for an outsider to be integrated with them. Therefore in my *happiness* of going to have a real visit, there is a nostalgic *sadness* in my heart". She realised she couldn't completely belong to the new China. Their ways were diverging and this must have caused her sorrow. On her

At Kaifeng 1979.

visit in 1959, they had really seen the activities in the countryside. But in 1975 and this time in 1979 she complained that they were being treated as tourists; they were not allowed to talk to the peasants. The local Party authorities arranged her entertainment and kept her isolated from the ordinary people. A group of ten peasant women who had known her as a child, came to see her but were not admitted.

They taught for two months at Fuzhou and at the end of July, a holiday was arranged for them. First they went to the Wuyi Mountains. On the way they stopped at Ruijin, the old Soviet capital in the 1930-34 period. Next morning they

came on by minibus, over the hills, a lovely ride to
Changting. They also visited Hetian, a little town 25 km.
away, where Hongying's elder sister lived after she married.
Hongying used to visit her there when she was a girl.

With some of her students at Fuzhou, 1979.

They remained five days in Changting. Staying in the same
Guest House, Hongying found an old woman, living in the
room below her. "Do you know who I am?" she asked; "I am
Liu Cifu! You were my favourite pupil!" She was the first
teacher Hongying had had in the Mission School, now 84
years old, with no wrinkles or white hair. She had been the
first wife of Fu Lianzhang, Mao's doctor and Minister of
Health under the Communists. She behaved in a very

affectionate way towards Hongying: "We have so much to talk about" she said. After the Long March, when she and Mao were in Changting, Mao asked her to take charge of the hospital there, partly for her own sake, but also for her husband's. The Changting Communist Party treasured her, invited her to stay in the Guest House and treated her with the greatest respect. She lived later in Shanghai with her children and grandchildren. But Hongying's high hopes for her hometown were somewhat damped on this occasion. The "deep-going political education" didn't seem to have penetrated this small town, shut off by its geographical situation, its mountains and transport difficulties. So Hongying had a double disappointment.

The first day, there had been a big family gathering in her old home with a grand dinner party. Special bowls of fine porcelain had been borrowed by the Party Committee to entertain them. "Are these the bowls you use every day?" she asked. She was angry! She was used to the plain thickish ones, like those they had in London. They were asked to stay in the Guest House and the family members came to see them there. Da-Sao (elder sister-in-law) spoke for them all and there was no discussion. All they wanted was more money. On her last visit, she had given each couple 100 yuan, so now they hoped for more. Hongying felt that all they cared for was money. The Party committee people surrounded them so that she couldn't speak intimately with her own family. Much too grand food and too much of it was provided.

Hongying is not a sentimental person but this time she was really upset. "Never again", she vowed. "I'll never come here again!"

Back in London, she got letters from her family members. "Come home" they wrote, "and you will solve all

133

our problems". But she knew there would only be new problems. These people were not truly liberated; they had no socialist ideas. She told her friends and colleagues at Fuzhou that she didn't want to go home any more because "my people have no political understanding and all the time is wasted on receptions and feasts. The Party isn't educating people there, it just provides feasts."

From 1979 to 1985, Hongying and Derek went back to China almost every year, for several months at a time, mostly teaching. Hongying ceased to teach in 1983; Derek in 1985. Now they are received as honoured guests. Old age is revered in China.

With science teachers studying English at Fuzhou, 1981.

The 1986 visit

Reunion at Nanchang, 1986.

Family group in the old home, December 1986.

Epilogue

Moving house; old age in Norwich

In the late 1980s many of the Edwardian houses in Holden Road, such as the Bryans', were sold for redevelopment, pulled down and replaced by blocks of flats. The environment was changing for the worse and this helped to provide the spur for Hongying and Derek to move out of London. With increasing years, Hongying was growing tired of entertaining the streams of visitors, English and Chinese, some welcome, others less so, who passed through and descended on them for varying periods. They were forever preparing meals, changing beds and making conversation. People were always asking for information or their opinions - about China, "as if we were the China office in London." Derek had a craving for the country - at least for a simpler life - they both wanted that.

By now, Hongying was conscious of her growing age, particularly her loss of memory. "Since December 1984, when I had a major operation, I have been ageing fast and in the process I have lost my memory and learning capacity - very distressing. But as it is the work of Nature, I don't complain or feel sad. I enjoy life and 'life' means comradeship of people with whom I come into contact." (To Alan and Johnie Simpson, 1988). Characteristically she doesn't 'moan' but accepts the inevitable. She often writes mockingly of "my old age syndrome", her diminishing sight and hearing.

"I am getting very old, very slow, forget where I have put things, waste time looking for them, forget how to write, often, the simplest Chinese or English words" (to Dr & Mrs

Rafael Acosta, 25 March 1989). These are common complaints of the old; it is her attitude which is different. "I think and think how very much I would like to join you...live to the end of life and work to the end of life", one of her friends, Eva Nappi, wrote to her in September 1988.

On 1st September 1988, they moved out of Finchley after over 32 years, back to Norwich, Derek's home town. "I always like a place with a history" Hongying often remarks, as she looks approvingly and with affection on some piece of the old city wall. They bought a house high above the city, with woods on one side and the beautiful spire of Norwich Cathedral rising above the house tops (few tower-blocks here!). At night the dark bowl is illuminated with hundreds of house lights, reproduced in the sky on clear nights, by stars. "A bird flies from the dark valleys into the lofty trees" she quotes from the ancient Chinese *Book of Songs*.

At Morston, North Norfolk, c. 1989.

The work for China had now inevitably become less. SACU had perforce given up its London headquarters for financial reasons, and a much diminished organisation had been set up in Cheltenham, with a few Branches around the country. The Library had found a home with the Great Britain-China Association, and the magazine 'China Now', had a separate existence. To tell the truth, China was no longer seen as the lodestar, the inspiration of the Left in Britain, possibly the world leader of the future. It had "faded into the light of common day" with its movement towards capitalism and the money motive (the aim, that everyone should own a car) and its abandonment of 'serving the people'.

Hongying would not admit this at first. Persistently optimistic and hopeful, she always said, "After many twists and turns, it will come right in the end. We must trust the people."

But 1989, the Tiananmen massacre, broke her spirit. However much we may blame the government leaders and their refusal to be humiliated, the workings of the media, the confusion, the fact remains that the People's Liberation Army was ordered to fire on unarmed students. They killed many of the leaders of the future.

Hongying wept for many days afterwards, and still weeps at times when she thinks of it. This is something that can't be wiped out.

They both retain links with their friends and (in Hongying's case) relatives in China, but their activities are more with the Quakers now, Hongying's old interest and support. Derek joined them and to his surprise was asked to be Joint Clerk of the Meeting. They have also provided a home for a succession of Chinese students and scholars who have lived with them in London and in Norwich. In this way,

On holday in Italy 1994.

By the river in Norwich, c.1994.

139

Hongying holding the photographer's baby, 1995.

at least in part, they made up for the lack of children. Derek has taken on ever more of the household chores including all the shopping. She pictures him "with bags over his shoulders, in his arms and hands, I often regard him as a camel!"

Hongying has also worked on the garden (a pretty and rather wild one). Her efforts were largely corrective: she addressed the rose-bushes like the educator she always was, cutting them back hard and training them "for their good". Looking back over the sum total of Hongying's long life, one may feel that in terms of worldly success, she didn't fulfil

At home in Norwich, 1995.

what might have been expected of her capabilities, but this is to forget the immense influence for good and the unfailing help she gave to all who crossed her path. Another Somervillian, Margaret Griffith, on being asked about her recollections of Hongying, replied, "I just remember that somehow or other, it came through to me that there was that element in her personality that one could only feel was heroic. We meet one or two people in our lifetime that we can put into that class - also one or two that one classes as saints, and between them they keep some sort of light burning." Hongying was not a saint; she would have rather disliked the epithet. But her name after all means in Chinese 'heroic'.

The gardener in Norwich, 1990.